MONSTER SCIENCE

Could Monsters Survive (and Thrive!) in the Real World?

Written by
Helaine Becker

Illustrated by
Phil McAndrew

KIDS CAN PRESS

To children's librarians everywhere — H.B.

For my brothers, Tyler and Ray, with whom I first started drawing monsters as a kid — P.M.

Text © 2016 Helaine Becker
Illustrations © 2016 Phil McAndrew

Acknowledgments
Thank you to the Ontario Arts Council for its support in the creation of this project. — H.B.

Kids Can Press acknowledges the financial support of the Government of Ontario, through the Ontario Media Development Corporation's Ontario Book Initiative; the Ontario Arts Council; the Canada Council for the Arts; and the Government of Canada, through the CBF, for our publishing activity.

Published in Canada by
Kids Can Press Ltd.
25 Dockside Drive
Toronto, ON M5A 0B5

Published in the U.S. by
Kids Can Press Ltd.
2250 Military Road
Tonawanda, NY 14150

www.kidscanpress.com

Edited by Katie Scott and Yasemin Uçar
Designed by Julia Naimska

This book is smyth sewn casebound.
Manufactured in Shenzhen, China, in 3/2016 by C & C Offset
CM 16 0 9 8 7 6 5 4 3 2 1

Library and Archives Canada Cataloguing in Publication

Becker, Helaine, 1961–, author
Monster science : could monsters survive (and thrive!) in the real world?
/ written by Helaine Becker ; illustrated by Phil McAndrew.

ISBN 978-1-77138-054-6 (bound)

1. Monsters — Juvenile literature. 2. Animals, Mythical — Juvenile literature.
3. Life sciences — Juvenile literature. I. McAndrew, Phil, 1985–, illustrator II. Title.

QL89.B43 2016   j001.944   C2015-907223-9

Kids Can Press is a **corus**™ Entertainment company

CONTENTS

Monsters Aren't Real ... or Are They???

Don't worry, you won't find any monsters living under your bed (unless you dread the dust bunny). But what if the terrifying creatures of your nightmares were indeed prowling the big, wide world beyond your blankie? Could they really exist? And if so, how? What proven scientific principles would allow Sasquatches to squash, vampires to vamp and zombies to zombify?

If you're thinking this book will tell you monsters are definitely, no-doubt-about-it real, you're out of luck. Instead, it will give you information to help you decide for yourself what is fact and what is fiction by exploring the worlds of supernatural monsters (those with uncanny powers) and cryptids (mysterious but wholly natural beasts). You'll unlock the scientific secrets that could explain how werewolves transform from human to beast and how bolt-necked Frankenstein could *z-z-zap!* to life. You'll visit the mysterious realms of sea monsters and the lairs of things that go bump in the night. And you'll discover how brain-eating fiends and bloodsucking beasts could possibly survive — and even thrive! — under the right conditions.

So be afraid. Be very, very afraid. You're about to come face-to-face with some of the scariest monsters on earth.

FRANKENSTEIN

Description: artificial man-monster brought to life by (*mwa ha ha!*) a mad scientist, rampaging on giant green feet through castles in Central Europe, Hollywood film studios — AND your worst nightmares.

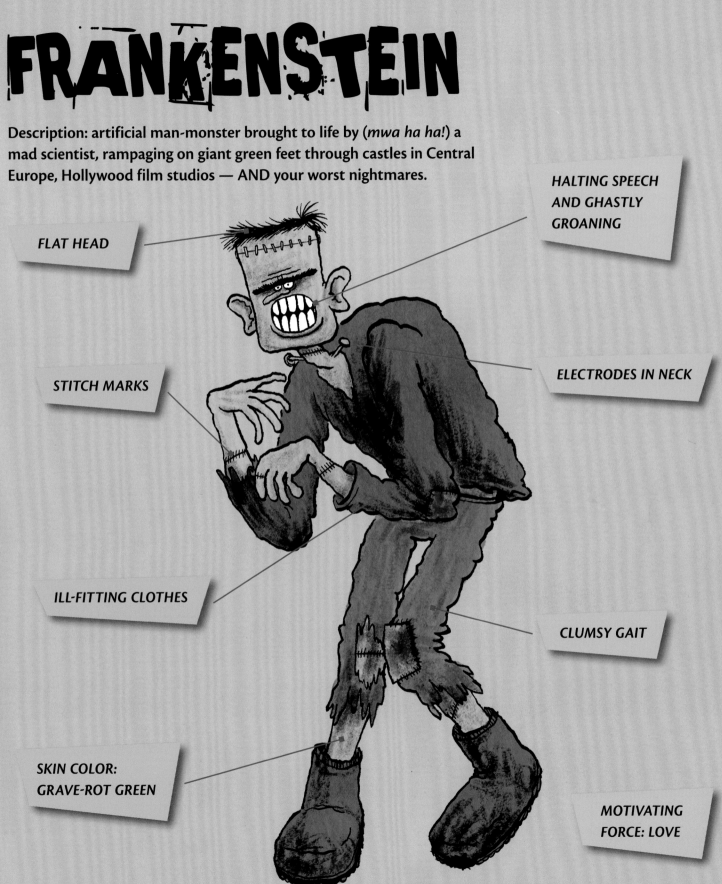

HALTING SPEECH AND GHASTLY GROANING

FLAT HEAD

ELECTRODES IN NECK

STITCH MARKS

ILL-FITTING CLOTHES

CLUMSY GAIT

SKIN COLOR: GRAVE-ROT GREEN

MOTIVATING FORCE: LOVE

The Story of Frankenstein

Imagine the weather's rotten and you and some friends are stuck indoors with nothing to do. How would you liven things up? Would you play a game? Tell a ghost story or two?

Whether you're at a sleepover, camping or chilling in a creepy castle, telling scary stories is an age-old way to pass the time. So when English poet Lord Byron and his friends were stuck in a gloomy house in Switzerland, that's just what he suggested. Each person would write a ghost story and read it aloud to the group. Mary Shelley was among those friends. Her spooky creation? The first draft of the novel *Frankenstein*.

Frankenstein; or, The Modern Prometheus was first published in 1818. Today, it is a must-read in schools around the world. It's also the inspiration for many popular films, TV shows, books and comics.

Shelley's bone-chilling story is about a scientist named Victor Frankenstein. He's obsessed with creating life. So Victor builds a man out of dead body parts and uses his science skills to zap it to life. But when his creation wakes, and Victor sees it in living, breathing, horrible action, Victor freaks out. He abandons it. Lonely and unloved, the man-made human acts out, sometimes in monstrous ways.

Monster Fact

At the same house party where Mary Shelley wrote *Frankenstein*, John Polidori wrote his famous short story "The Vampyre." (See page 26.)

Monster Fact

In Greek mythology, Prometheus was one of the Titans who created the universe. He molded humankind out of clay and was later punished for stealing fire from the other gods and giving it to humans.

LONELY MONSTERS

Many "popular" villains have suffered from loneliness. Consider these notorious fictional examples:

- Lord Voldemort, the evil Dark Lord in the Harry Potter stories, was an orphan. From an early age, he was denied parental affection. He grew up isolated and alone.

- The Penguin, one of Batman's enemies, grew evil after being rejected by his parents and bullied for his strange appearance and obsession with birds.

- The Grinch lived far from society, isolated from everyone and everything except his dog. His loneliness turned him bitter, making his heart "two sizes too small."

Can loneliness really turn you into a monster? Scientific research suggests it could. Everybody feels lonely sometimes, but feeling lonely for a long, long time actually transforms the brain. Those changes can make people less outgoing. Lonely people find it harder to enjoy the things that typically make others happy. Extremely lonely people feel pleasure when they see other people not getting along. That can make them want to stir up trouble.

The Age of Enlightenment

Where did Mary Shelley get her ideas for *Frankenstein*? The eighteenth century — when Shelley was born — was considered part of the Enlightenment because many scientific principles were being discovered at the time. Electricity — what it was and how it worked — was a hot topic.

Mary Shelley knew about these ideas. She was well-educated and especially interested in science. She also knew lots of famous scientists, including Sir Humphry Davy, a well-known electrical researcher and scientist of the era.

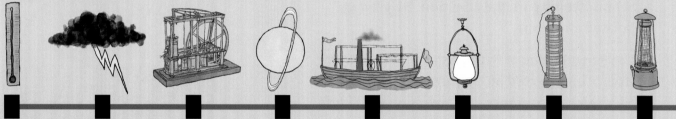

1717 Gabriel Fahrenheit invents the first mercury thermometer.

1752 Benjamin Franklin proves lightning is electrical. (See page 13.)

1769 James Watt's steam engine propels the Industrial Revolution.

1781 William Herschel discovers Uranus.

1790 John Fitch invents the first successful steamboat.

1792 William Murdoch invents gas lighting.

1800 Alessandro Volta builds the first battery. (See page 10.)

1809 Humphry Davy creates the first electric lamp.

Franken-frog

Around 1780, Luigi Galvani made an important discovery. When his assistant touched a metal scalpel to a dead frog's exposed nerve, its leg jumped!

Galvani believed that electricity ran through the frog's nerves. If this was true, he wondered, could electricity be the source of life? Scientists did a series of experiments to find the answer. Electric shocks were even applied to victims of drowning in attempts to bring them back to life.

These experiments were not only interesting to scientists. They also became a source of "edutainment" for ordinary people. Traveling exhibitions toured Europe to show the effects of electricity. One of the showmen was Giovanni Aldini (Galvani's nephew). In 1803, at a famous prison called Newgate, Aldini shocked the corpse of an executed murderer. The corpse sat up! Many spectators believed the corpse was coming back to life. It wasn't. The shock just made the corpse's muscles contract, like in Galvani's frog. The question of whether electricity was the source of life remained open.

WHAT IS ELECTRICITY ANYWAY?

Everything in the universe is made up of tiny particles called atoms. The atoms are made up of even tinier particles called protons, electrons and neutrons.

The protons and electrons have electrical charges. Protons have a positive charge and electrons have a negative charge. (Neutrons have no charge.) Particles that have the same electrical charge repel each other (push each other away). Particles with opposite charges attract each other (pull each other together).

Protons and neutrons form the center, or nucleus, of the atom, and electrons whirl around the nucleus. The electrons interact with particles belonging to other atoms. They repel particles that have negative charges and attract particles that have positive charges. Sometimes an electron will break free and move from one atom to another. That motion is electricity.

When there are a bunch of atoms together and electrons are moving from one atom to another in the same direction, it's called an electrical current. In the same way that a current of water has more force than a single water droplet, an electrical current has more force than a single electron. A current can literally push particles around so they do work, like light up light bulbs or make motors spin.

Some materials are made of atoms that lose electrons more easily than others. These materials conduct electricity better, because more electrons are moving from atom to atom. Copper is one of these materials, which is why electrical wires are made from this metal.

9

Galvani vs. Volta

Galvani believed that the electricity making the frog's leg jump came from within the frog itself. Another Italian scientist, Alessandro Volta, thought differently. He believed that the electricity came from a chemical reaction between the two metals found in Galvani's scalpel. A scientific feud broke out. Observers divided into two camps. But who was right, Galvani or Volta?

In 1800, Volta invented a device called the voltaic pile. It was made of alternating stacks of zinc and copper separated by paper soaked in salt water. The chemical reaction between the metals generated electricity, like Galvani's scalpel.

The voltaic pile was the first battery people had ever seen. It also proved Volta right. He was able to show that the electrical activity Galvani observed didn't come from the frog.

Q: How does Frankenstein sit in his chair?
A: Bolt upright!

THE VOLTAIC PILE: HOW IT WORKS

Each element has a unique number of electrons. That makes them behave differently from each other. Some elements, such as copper, like to give away electrons, while others, such as zinc, like to grab them.

Salt water contains a special kind of charged particle called an ion. Ions have an unequal number of electrons and protons and freely exchange electrons with one another. They also help electrons in nearby materials move more freely.

A voltaic pile is made up of alternating stacks of copper and zinc, separated by cardboard or felt soaked in brine (salt water). The zinc on one end of the stack wants to grab electrons. The copper on the other end wants to give away electrons. The brine-soaked separators act like bridges, carrying the electrons from the copper to the zinc. Those moving electrons are an electrical current!

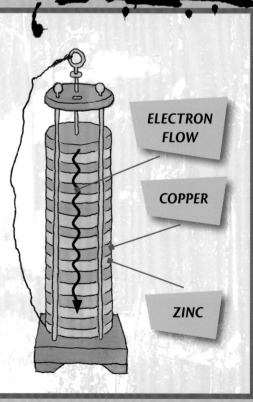

ELECTRON FLOW

COPPER

ZINC

The "Mad" Scientist

During the Enlightenment, the pace of scientific discovery was lightning-fast. People worried it might be too fast — and go too far. Discussions about the ethics (the rights and wrongs) of science were fierce and frequent.

Mary Shelley's novel tackled some of these ethical questions. Her story makes readers think about who the real monster is. Is it the doctor's shocking creation or the egocentric doctor himself?

Dr. Frankenstein represented the dangers of this new scientific age so well that he became the model for mad scientist characters in scores of books, movies and comic strips.

Are you mad for mad scientists? Hollywood is! Compare how scientists and science were portrayed in a thousand horror films made between 1930 and 1990.

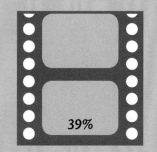

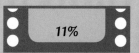

30%

39%

11%

30% of movies featured mad scientists and their creations as the villains.

39% of movies featured scientific research unleashing a dangerous threat.

11% of movies featured scientists as heroes.

MAD SCIENTIST — FACT OR FICTION?

There may be a scientific explanation for the legend of the mad scientist. Consider the case of Isaac Newton, one of the most famous and influential scientists of all time, who endured a period of temporary madness.

Newton, it turns out, experimented with the toxic chemical mercury. He may have given himself mercury poisoning! High levels of the toxic element turned up in his hair samples when they were tested many years after his death. Symptoms of mercury poisoning include irritability, fits of anger, anxiety, paranoia, restlessness and violent, irrational behavior.

Franken-then vs. Franken-now

When Mary Shelley wrote *Frankenstein*, no one knew whether her story could come true. Today, we have a much deeper understanding of how the human body works and can answer some of the most perplexing questions.

Can Electricity Wake the Dead?

According to the legend, the Frankenstein monster was brought to life by a jolt of electricity. But can electricity really be life-giving?

It depends on both how long a person has been dead and the cause of death. Red blood cells carry oxygen throughout the body. Our brains and bodies cannot work without this precious element. Brain cells starved of oxygen will begin to die in as little as four minutes.

Imagine, now, that someone has suffered a heart attack — the muscles in her heart have stopped working. Oxygen-rich blood is no longer being pumped through the body. Unless the heart begins pumping again, and quickly, she will die.

Until 1959, there was no way to restart a stopped heart without opening up the body. Now, externally applied electricity can do it. It can artificially make heart muscles contract, just like Galvani's frog legs, causing blood and its cargo of oxygen to get moving again.

So as long as there is little or no tissue decay or brain damage, the "dead" — that is, a person without vital signs — *can* be revived.

Shocking a stopped heart isn't a surefire restarter, though. How long the heart has been stopped makes a difference. So does how warm or cold the person was when her heart stopped. And restarting a heart that has stopped for a few minutes is a far cry from reanimating a dug-up corpse.

Monster Fact

The first recorded accidental electrocution (besides lightning strikes) occurred in 1879 when a stage carpenter in Lyon, France, touched a 250-volt wire.

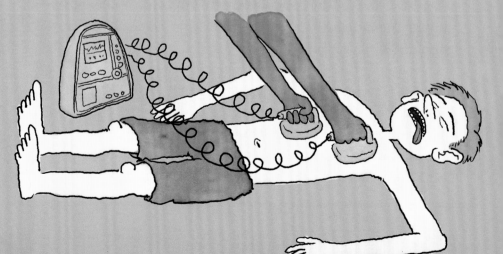

A machine called a portable manual defibrillator is standard first-aid equipment found in ambulances, public buildings, airplanes and trains. The machine applies an electrical shock to restart heart muscle in the event of a medical emergency.

Electricity in the Body

It's said that Benjamin Franklin discovered electricity by flying a kite in a storm. He was incredibly lucky. He could have received the shock of his life — or death. A strong electric shock can kill you. It can interfere with nerve cells' electrical activity. Depending on how severe the shock, these nerve cells might stop being able to communicate. Vital functions such as breathing can stop completely.

Remember how Luigi Galvani thought that electricity was generated by the tissues inside the frog? And how he was proven wrong by Volta and his voltaic pile?

That's not the whole story. It turns out that *both* men were right!

Volta was right because the electrical current generated by Galvani's scalpel did not come from the frog.

But Galvani was also right. It wasn't until the twentieth century that technology had advanced enough to prove it, but living cells *do* generate electricity. Like mini voltaic piles, nerve cells have the ability to convert chemical energy to electrical energy.

The Neuron Race

Your nervous system is your body's main communication system. It works using both chemical and electrical energy to deliver messages throughout the body.

The nervous system is made up of billions of nerve cells called neurons. Each neuron has a "control center" made of dendrites, which receive signals from other cells, and axons, which send electrical signals to other cells. Your brain is made up of about 86 billion neurons.

Neurons communicate with each other through a kind of electrochemical relay race. The sequence works like this:

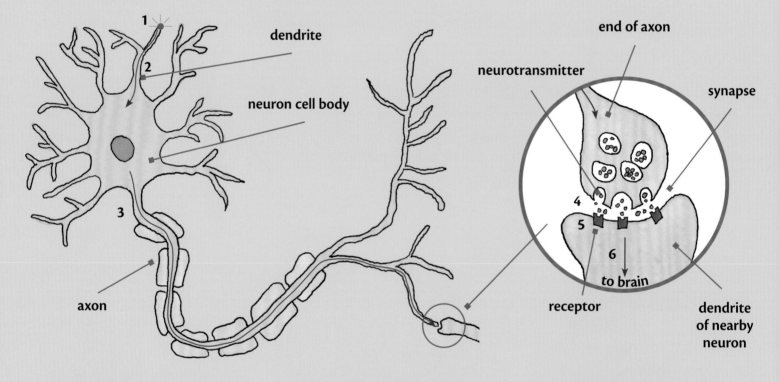

1. *A fly lands on your arm. The tickle causes a sensory neuron to react. Its branch-like dendrites receive the electrical signal.*

2. *The signal travels like a wave to the neuron's cell body.*

3. *The electrical wave continues down the length of the axon.*

4. *When the signal reaches the end of the axon, chemical messengers called neurotransmitters are released. The neurotransmitters travel across the synapse — the gap between two neurons.*

5. *Receptors on the dendrites of a nearby neuron receive the neurotransmitters, setting off another round of electrical nerve impulses.*

6. *The process repeats itself until the message arrives at its destination, the brain. Finally, the message is delivered: "There is a fly on my arm!"*

ELECTRICITY AND YOUR MUSCLES

Your muscles also rely on electricity to work. Just like in nerve cells, electrical waves cause shape and chemical changes along the entire muscle fiber. Those changes cause muscles to contract. As the muscle shortens, it pulls on your bones, moving them so you can bend your arm or kick a ball.

The heart muscle has its own electrical generator, called the sinoatrial (SA) node. The SA node produces regular bursts of electricity that cause heart muscle to contract approximately 60 to 100 times per minute. That rhythmic contraction is known as your pulse, or heartbeat.

In some people's hearts, the SA node doesn't fire properly. So an electrical device called a pacemaker is inserted near the left shoulder. If the heart falters, the pacemaker emits a tiny electrical pulse to restore its normal rhythm and prevent a heart attack. Today more than three million people have electronic pacemakers.

Sensory vs. Motor Neurons

There are three main types of neurons in the body. Sensory neurons carry messages from your skin, muscles and glands to your brain and spinal cord. They are information-oriented. Their messages contain data about the body and the environment, such as, "I detect a tickle on my left elbow."

Interneurons are found in the brain and spinal cord, and connect sensory neurons to motor neurons. The interneurons are decision-oriented. They take the data from sensory neurons and interpret it. For example, they may decide the tickle on your elbow is a fly. They then decide what the best course of action is and give an instruction to the motor neurons, such as, "Contract muscles so right hand will swat fly away."

Motor neurons carry messages from the brain and spinal cord to your skin, muscles and glands. They are action-oriented. Their messages contain instructions, such as, "Contract this muscle."

Monster Fact

Galvani thought electricity was the force that made living things live. But what is life, exactly? That's not as simple a question as it sounds. In fact, to this day, scientists can't agree on a definition!

Can You Mix and Match Parts to Build a Whole New Person?

In the Frankenstein story, Dr. Frankenstein puts together an entirely new "person" using bits and pieces taken from other people. Could you do this in real life? Not exactly. But modern doctors and scientists can and *do* use donated human organs to help living people live healthier lives. And using a laboratory technique called genetic engineering, they can also stitch together new strands of DNA to create organisms with special new traits!

Organ Transplantation

Organs from still-living or recently deceased people can be sewn into — or onto — living people to replace damaged or non-functional organs. This helps their bodies function better and can keep them alive longer. You can also attach other body parts, such as hands. Entire faces have even been transplanted onto people whose own were badly disfigured.

But you can't just dig up a cemetery and take parts from any old cadaver to use for organ transplants. The transplant procedure is complicated and requires a team of medical specialists and consent.

How Organ Transplant Works

1. Organs are obtained from a person who has given prior consent. The organ donor can be either alive or dead. Living donors can donate organs such as one of their lungs or kidneys, since people normally have two of each. They can also donate part of their liver, since livers can grow back. Some people sign an organ donor card to agree to donate organs after their death. Many different organs can be donated after death. One donor might help up to 50 people!

2. Donated organs are preserved using artificial ventilation and/or refrigeration until transplant time. They can survive for 5 to 30 hours, depending on the type of organ.

3. The organs are matched to a list of possible recipients who need them. A match is made when the donor and the recipient are compatible — they have to have the same body size and blood type. The transplant team also looks at the recipient's health to make sure he is strong enough for the procedure, and how long he has been waiting for an organ.

4. After the organ is transplanted, the recipient will remain under medical care for the rest of his life. Because the organ is not natural to that person, his immune system will try to reject it. Anti-rejection medication is required to keep this from happening. A transplant patient may also be more vulnerable to infections and experience other health complications as a result of the surgery.

Monster Fact

The world's first successful live-donor organ transplant was performed in 1954. Ronald Herrick donated a kidney to his twin brother, Richard, who was dying of kidney disease.

A VERY GRAVE MATTER

In Mary Shelley's day, organ transplants were not possible. But corpses were regularly stolen from cemeteries. It may sound downright disgusting, but to this day, doctors learn about anatomy from dissecting cadavers. Before organ donation programs existed, most cadavers used in medical schools were obtained from prisons — usually the bodies of executed criminals. But there weren't enough of those to go around. So anatomy teachers hired people to dig up graves and steal the bodies from them. They were called body snatchers.

The most famous body snatchers of all time were William Burke and William Hare, who lived and worked in Edinburgh, Scotland. In order to make enough money from their trade, they sometimes supplemented their income — by murdering people!

They'd then sell the bodies for cold hard cash. Burke's last victim was murdered on Halloween night in 1828, but Burke didn't have time to move the body without getting caught. One of his lodgers discovered the corpse in a spare room the next day. Hare testified against Burke. Burke was convicted of murder and hanged in 1829. His body was publicly dissected by anatomists.

William Burke kept a notebook in which he recorded his murderous activity. These are some of the entries:

Christmas 1827 — *Sold the body of Donald the pensioner, in Surgeon Square, for £7, 10. Paid William Hare, Tanner's Close, £4, 5. For myself, £3, 5.*

April 2 — *Sold the woman from Gilmerton for £9. Paid William Hare foresaid, £4. Paid a porter 5 … For myself £4, 10s.*

An iron cage was sometimes placed around a newly dug grave by family members to prevent the body from being stolen. Sometimes people sat watch over the grave for several weeks or set booby traps to catch body snatchers in the act.

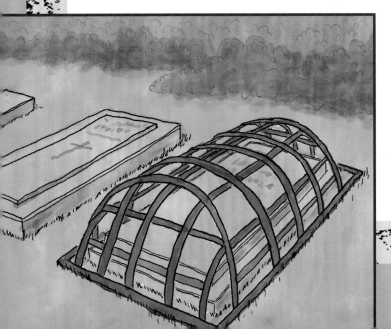

Mix 'n' Match: Genetic Engineering

Imagine you have a bean plant that produces a huge crop of delicious beans every year. People love to eat them. But so do insects! Meanwhile, you have another plant that isn't attractive to pests. Wouldn't it be great if you could take the pest resistance from Plant B and put it into Plant A?

You'd have a yummy crop of beans without having to share your harvest with bugs.

In the mid-1800s, Gregor Mendel discovered that this was possible in his famous experiment with peas (see page 75). But people have been doing this for thousands of years. They cross — or, in the case of animals, mate — different species to develop traits we want, such as delicious fruit, stronger stems or domesticated animals. It's kind of like how Dr. Frankenstein pieced together different parts to make his monster. But it takes a very long time and lots of hard work!

Genetic engineering is a scientific technique that speeds up this process. It means building something with genes. In a lab, scientists chemically "snip" genes from an organism, such as Plant A. They then add new genes, such as the pest resistance gene from Plant B, directly into the snipped genes. The resulting plant, a genetically modified organism (GMO), that grows from those cells will now have traits from both Plant A and Plant B.

Genetic engineering can be very helpful. GMO bacteria can produce insulin for people with diabetes, and GMO corn can resist common plant-eating pests. But genetic engineering also has risks. Some fear that GMO crops could "escape" into the wild and contaminate other species. Others worry about the effects of GMO foods on our health.

Monster Fact

Genes carry the information that determines an organism's traits — in humans, these are the characteristics you inherit from your parents, such as brown eyes or green eyes, curly hair or straight hair.

Pretty Kitty?

Glow-in-the-dark cats were created by researchers in South Korea by inserting genes from fluorescent coral into feline egg cells. The resulting offspring glow red under ultraviolet light.

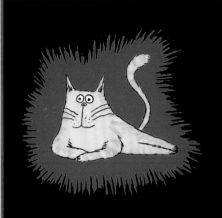

Spectacular Spider-goat?

Genetically engineered goats can now produce milk that contains spider silk. When the goats are milked, the silk can be separated from the rest of the milk and the ultra-strong fibers can be used to make bulletproof vests or artificial tendons.

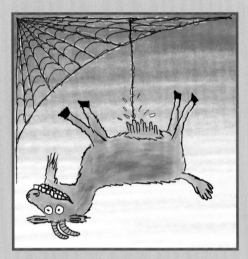

Robots — Modern-Day Frankensteins?

The term *robot* means "artificial human." That makes the Frankenstein monster the world's first representation of a robot.

But can robots think and feel, like Frankenstein did? Are robots alive? Consider these boundary-busting creations:

Nanobots are miniature robots. Some are made of computerized parts attached to bacteria. That makes nanobots real-life, organism-machine hybrids.

Robotic engineers are also creating robot brains that can think and feel. Some of these "brains" exhibit curiosity. They learn from mistakes. They can be creative and reproduce themselves.

Because of these abilities, many scientists today consider some robots to be alive. Others think robots will reach that stage very soon.

GMOs ON FILM

With all the controversy surrounding genetic engineering, it's no wonder it has become such a popular theme in movies. In recent *Spider-Man* and *Iron Man* movies, for example, genetic changes give superheroes their powers. In other stories, like *Jurassic Park* or *The Incredible Hulk*, however, genetic experimentation unleashes dangerous creatures that can cause great harm. Interestingly, Stan Lee, the creator of *The Incredible Hulk*, said his character was inspired by two nineteenth-century novels: *The Strange Case of Dr. Jekyll and Mr. Hyde* and — yes — *Frankenstein*!

Monster Fact

To protect robots now and in the future, robot rights activists have written a Robot Ethics Charter — a kind of Robot Bill of Rights!

Build Your Own Monster

After reading this chapter, you probably know even more about creating life than Dr. Frankenstein did! So are you ready to build your own monster? Examine each body part below and decide if the statement on it is true or false. Then check your monster-score to find out how you rate as a mad scientist.

 1. Scientists agree on how to define life.

 2. Mary Shelley was married to a doctor named Igor Polidori.

 3. Loneliness can make a person more antisocial.

 4. The term *robot* means "artificial human."

5. Electrons moving in the same direction are called a synapse.

6. Lightning is composed of electricity.

 7. Luigi Galvani made dead frogs' legs jump and twitch.

 8. Scientists have created glow-in-the-dark cats by combining genes from coral with genes from a cat.

9. Nerve cells use both electrical and chemical signals to send and receive messages.

10. Body snatching was once a solid career option.

0–2 parts   LUIGI GALVANI — You are a rock-star scientist. You can make a dead frog dance with a *z-z-zap*! of electricity, but have not yet mastered bringing it fully back to life. Please brush your hair.

3–6 parts   ISAAC NEWTON — You are a very mad scientist. You can build monsters using nothing but moth wings and spit. And a falling apple (*BONK!*), of course.

7–10 parts   DR. FRANKENSTEIN HIMSELF!!! — You are the ultimate mad scientist. You don't need to build a monster ... because (*mwa ha ha*) you *are* one!!!

Answers: 1. False, 2. False, 3. True, 4. True, 5. False, 6. True, 7. True, 8. True, 9. True, 10. True

VAMPIRE

Description: once-normal humans who lost their lives and gained immortality after being bitten by another vampire. Some say they feed only on blood and can't stand the sun. Others just say — RUN!

DEATHLY PALLOR

WIDOW'S PEAK

HYPNOTIC EYES

FANGS

KEEN FASHION SENSE

CAPE (OPTIONAL)

COFFIN FOR DAYTIME SNOOZING

OBSESSED WITH COUNTING

Demonic Diseases

You're playing softball in the Lunchtime League at school. You whack the ball, round the bases and score the winning run! But ouch! You've scraped your palms sliding into home. The school nurse stops the bleeding and cleans the wound so it won't get infected.

Count yourself lucky — and not just for winning the game. In the past, those scrapes on your palms may have gotten you into another kind of scrape. For most of human history, no one knew what caused illness. Germs, for example, weren't even discovered until the nineteenth century. So when people got sick — with a fever from an infected scrape, for example — it was often thought that they had sinned or were possessed by evil spirits.

To cure them, healers tried to find ways to remove the demons. One method was bloodletting: scraping or cutting the skin to let blood — and demons — flow out. Leeches (a kind of worm that feeds on blood) were frequently placed on patients' skin to suck out the evil spirits from their blood.

Starting with the Egyptians about three thousand years ago, bloodletting was the most common medical technique used around the world, although it frequently made patients worse, not better. Until the eighteenth century, many Europeans got bled regularly to prevent disease — even when they weren't sick! The practice is still performed in many parts of the world, including Asia and the Middle East.

Since removing blood "released" demons, consuming blood was believed to do the opposite. Blood-drinking creatures naturally became feared and hated, and featured in scary stories!

Monster Fact

Long ago, barbers commonly performed bloodletting. The red-and-white striped barber pole, still seen today, represents the red blood and the white fabric that staunched the blood flow.

The Heart of the Vampire Empire

The first written mention of vampires is found in an eleventh-century document in Old Russian. In it, an evil prince is referred to as *Upir Lichy*, or "wicked vampire." By the 1600s, the word *upir* had gradually morphed into *vampyr* or *vampir*.

The name spread to Bulgaria and Romania, where vampire myths were most deeply embedded. There, ancient Slavic legends told of ghosts that needed fresh blood to return to the underworld. From about 1600 on, though, people believed that corpses, not just ghosts, could rise from the grave to feed on blood — especially human blood!

To stop the marauding corpses, villagers would dig up recently buried bodies, expose them to sunlight and stab them through the heart.

Stories about real-life vampires spread down to Italy. One "vampire" from Venice was buried with a brick in her mouth to prevent her from biting new victims when she rose from the grave.

The Vampire Controversy

The Enlightenment (see page 8) was a period of great progress and discovery. But in Central Europe, the eighteenth century was also a dark and frightening time. Years of recurring plague had killed thousands of Europeans and left others weakened, superstitious and scared. People were desperate for answers and suddenly began reporting vampire sightings and telling hair-raising tales of dead relatives rising from their graves. This bloodthirsty episode is known as the eighteenth-century vampire controversy.

Authorities took the reports seriously. They investigated the claims by digging up fresh graves of suspected vampires and examining them for signs of nighttime marauding. Observers believed they had found a vampire when a corpse had a rosy complexion, a bloody mouth or long, fresh nails — all normal occurrences. If the corpse was discovered in a strange position (also normal), it was considered further proof that it had risen for a midnight snack. The investigators burned these corpses and drove stakes through their hearts in very public "executions" — of already dead bodies!

Monster Fact

Elizabeth Bathory was a Transylvanian noblewoman who was just like a real vampire! She drank blood to stay young and tortured and killed hundreds of people before she was tried and convicted for murder.

The Scientific Revolution

The eighteenth-century vampire controversy came at the end of a 150-year period known as the Scientific Revolution. This unprecedented period of learning led to many medical advances. Scientists understood for the first time how internal organs, such as the heart and lungs, worked. They started identifying diseases and figuring out what caused them. They conducted experiments on different cures to find out what really worked. These early experiments revealed that many old beliefs — such as demons causing disease — were false, and that many cures — such as bloodletting — did more harm than good. The Scientific Revolution laid the foundation for modern medicine.

Harvey's Heart

William Harvey was an English physician who lived and worked during the Scientific Revolution. He studied the human body in great detail. He used precise measurements and conducted countless experiments to determine the function of the heart, arteries and veins and how they work together to circulate blood through the body — what we call the circulatory system. He proved that the heart is the central organ of the circulatory system, not the liver, as was previously thought.

Harvey's findings were controversial in his day, but today we know his ideas about the circulatory system were right!

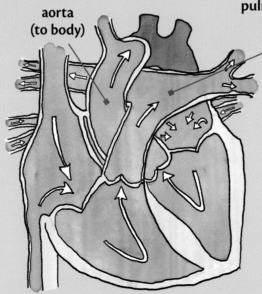

aorta
(to body)

pulmonary artery
(to lungs)

Because of William Harvey, we now know exactly how the heart pumps blood through the body.

The left side of the heart (red) pumps oxygen-rich blood through the aorta to the arteries throughout your body. When the blood reaches the tiniest blood vessels, called capillaries, the blood transfers oxygen directly to individual cells.

The blood travels back to the heart through the veins, picking up carbon dioxide, a waste product, on the way. The right side of the heart (blue) pumps blood to the lungs through the pulmonary artery. The lungs release the carbon dioxide when you exhale, and replenish the blood with oxygen when you inhale.

24

THE STORY OF BLOOD

We now know a lot more about blood — and how it works — than in William Harvey's day. Blood is made up of four main parts. Each performs an important role in keeping your body healthy.

- Red blood cells, or erythrocytes, give blood its crimson hue. They carry oxygen to all the cells of your body.

- White blood cells, or leukocytes, defend the body against infections. They destroy viruses or other intruders by surrounding them and digesting them.

- Platelets, or thrombocytes, can group together to form sticky clumps. They also help to produce strands of a protein called fibrin. The clumped platelets and tangles of fibrin stop bleeding. Inside the body, they are called clots. On your skin, they are called scabs.

- Plasma is a yellowish liquid. It carries the different types of blood cells, along with nutrients, hormones and proteins, to all parts of the body. Plasma is mostly made up of water.

Most blood cells are made in the bone marrow: the soft, fatty inner parts of your long bones. Others are produced in your lymph nodes, spleen and the thymus gland in your chest. Your body makes two million new red blood cells every second!

Monster Fact

Blood makes the entire trip around the body three times every minute!

white blood cell

blood vessel

red blood cell

platelet

plasma

Dracula Awakes

Thanks to the Scientific Revolution, investigators were able to use newly discovered facts about the human body and disease to put a stake in the heart of the vampire controversy. They squashed superstitious beliefs by proving that the strange phenomena in suspected vampires' graves (such as rosy cheeks and bloody mouths) were actually normal processes of decay.

But no one could keep a good vampire story down. In 1816, John Polidori and a few friends, including Mary Shelley and Lord Byron, wrote some horror stories for fun (see page 6). Polidori published his short story called "The Vampyre" in 1819.

Until this time, vampires were imagined to be little more than crude beasts. Polidori's story changed that. His vampire was elegant and handsome. A craze for all things vampire swept London and Paris, and vampire stories and plays would continue to haunt European entertainment for the rest of the century.

Influenced by Polidori's story, author Bram Stoker stoked the European appetite for bloodthirsty beings with his novel *Dracula* in 1897. It portrayed this now-iconic vampire: the Transylvanian Count Dracula who avoids sunlight, changes shape into animals, lacks a reflection and sleeps in a coffin.

This versatile version of the vampire story has become a staple of Hollywood movies, TV shows and Halloween costumes.

The dark, handsome and mysterious poet Lord Byron was a lot like John Polidori's vampire!

Monster Fact

The word *dracul* means "dragon" in Romanian.

Bran Castle, the alleged home of Bram Stoker's Count Dracula, is the number-one tourist attraction in Romania with more than half a million visitors each year.

How to Stop a Vampire

Vampires like Dracula may acquire superstrength when they transform from regular mortals. That makes them very hard to fend off. Modern vampire experts offer some suggestions on how to defeat a vampire if you ever meet one:

- The best way to kill a vampire is to stab it through the heart with a stake. Even vampires can't live with a broken heart.

- Dragging a vampire into the sun can cause its skin to sizzle and burn, giving it a suntan to die for.

- Holy water or crucifixes can also have a nasty effect on a vampire's skin. But you would need a lot of holy water to do major damage. Otherwise, expect a very damp, and very annoyed, bloodsucker.

- A whiff of garlic acts like a spritz of vampire repellent. So you might consider fashioning some garlicky accessories.

- You can kill a vamp with fire, but it will have to turn him to ash before his tissue regenerates. A blowtorch might do the trick. Don't forget the dustpan.

So if Dracula comes knocking, there's no need to cower under the covers. With your anti-vamp toolkit at the ready, you'll have what it takes to send Drac packing!

Vampire Fact vs. Vampire Fiction

According to lore, vampires possess some seriously strange characteristics. Were these legendary traits just the stuff of scary stories? Or could these creepy creature features really exist?

The Dracula Diet

The details of vampires' lives may vary, but vamps all share one key trait: they drink blood. But could someone really live on blood alone?

Even though we humans need blood in our veins to live, blood has a few problems as a food source. Blood does contain many nutrients. But it also contains substances that are harmful for us. One of them is iron, a metal that gives red blood cells their color. Although we need that iron to carry oxygen to the cells of our bodies, excess iron can cause liver disease and damage the nervous system. In large quantities, it's actually *toxic*. So even though it sounds scrumdiddlyumptious, forget about eating nothing but blood pudding, blood pudding, blood pudding for the rest of your life.

It is possible, however, that some people could adapt to more iron in their diets. After all, many animals with blood diets manage just fine. Even so, blood doesn't contain all the nutrients human bodies need for tip-top health. Even vampires would have to eat their vegetables.

Monster Fact

Vampires first got fangs in 1845, when a story about Varney the Vampire read, "With a plunge he seizes her neck in his fang-like teeth."

Monster Fact

Vampire bats were unknown in medieval Europe. They got their name from the human vampire, not the other way around.

Real-Life Bloodsuckers

Vampires are one-hundred-percent real — in the animal kingdom, at least. There are many animals that live entirely on blood. Others eat a variety of foods, but still make blood a big part of their diets. Meet these real-life bloodsuckers … if you dare.

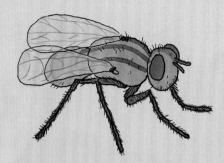

Vampire bats use their fangs like can openers to poke holes in the tough hides of their (mostly animal) victims, leaving a distinctive double-fang bite mark. Then, using their tongues, they lap the blood that seeps out.

Vampire finches are found in the Galapagos Islands, where there isn't a lot of fresh water. So whenever they are thirsty, they jab their beaks into the butt-feathers of another bird called a booby and take a long, refreshing drink — of its blood.

Flies poke, bite or scratch a wound in their victims' skin. Then they use a spongy pad in their mouths to soak up the blood. They generally leave a little poo and pee behind while they feed, as a calling card.

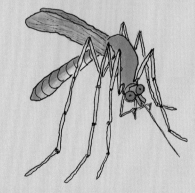

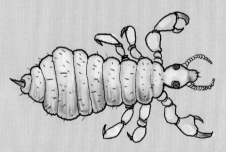

Leeches have suction cups at each end of their bodies to attach themselves to your flesh. An ooze of mucus keeps their grip firm while they use their circular, sawlike teeth to make a Y-shaped incision in your skin. As they fill up on your blood, they may expand up to nine times their original size!

Mosquitoes come armed with a long, sharp beak called a proboscis. It acts like a sword to pierce through skin. The insects inject a substance into the wound to keep blood from clotting. Then they use their proboscis like a straw to suck blood until they've had their fill.

Head lice like to grab on to your hair, close to your scalp, and stay there for their whole lives — about 30 days. When they eat, they use a part of their mouths called stylets to saw through your scalp and suck your blood.

How Would Vampires Suck Your Blood?

Vampires are often shown slurping supper from their victims' necks. That makes sense, scientifically speaking. Two of the largest arteries in your body, the carotid arteries, are located on either side of your neck. They carry oxygen-rich blood from your heart to your head and brain. Blood from these arteries would be highly nutritious for brainy vampires.

Q: What is a vampire's favorite fruit?

A: A neck-tarine

Take a Bite!

You've probably seen dogs, cats or even snakes with sharp fangs. But most people don't have them. Our own chompers have evolved so that we can chow down on many different kinds of food without needing pointy piercers. The squarish teeth (incisors) at the front of our mouths are good for biting hard foods, such as carrots. The bumpy molars at the back are good for grinding up tough foods, such as meat or nuts. Our canine (cuspid) teeth are the most fang-like, and are indeed used for piercing. Think apples, though, not necks.

Some people, however, may be born with a rare genetic condition called hypohidrotic ectodermal dysplasia. It can cause a narrow jaw, sparse hair and thick, dark skin below the eyes. It can also make teeth grow sharp and pointy. The teeth can look very much like a vampire's fangs!

A CASE OF VAMPIRE-ITIS

The disease that creates fangs isn't the only condition that might make you resemble a vampire. Some historians think other diseases with vampire-like symptoms could have been behind the sightings during the eighteenth-century vampire controversy. While none of these diseases cause people to actually drink blood, they do make people look or act a lot like vampires:

- Tuberculosis, a bacterial infection of the lungs, causes sufferers to appear pale, avoid bright light and cough up blood. If some blood accidentally remained on the lips, the patient might look like she'd been drinking the red stuff.

- Some forms of Plague (see page 60) break down lung tissue, so blood could appear on the lips with every breath.

- Rabies (see pages 63 and 79) can cause people to behave in aggressive ways and to fear light, water or mirrors. The most common transmitter of rabies in the world is stray dogs. In North America, it's bats.

- Xeroderma pigmentosum causes the skin to blister when it comes into contact with the sun's ultraviolet rays.

Sufferers must avoid sunlight or risk disfigurement. They are even at risk for early death from skin cancer.

- Porphyria (see page 79) is a group of genetic disorders that can cause sensitivity to sunlight, changes in skin color and urine to turn red, as if from drinking blood.

Wherever some of these diseases took hold, death rates would suddenly soar. It's easy to see how, without an understanding of infectious diseases, terrified people could start to believe in real-life vampires!

Could a Person Really Live Forever?

One of the most alluring things about vampires is their reputation for immortality. Even if you're convinced a human could adapt to a blood diet, that doesn't account for this special talent of living forever. If vampires were real, how would they manage to overcome that pesky obstacle called death?

Say hello to HeLa, a strain of human cells that have been cultured in petri dishes around the world since 1951. The cells were obtained from the cervix of a woman with cancer named Henrietta Lacks. (HeLa cells are named after the first two letters of her first and last name.) Although Henrietta died of her disease, the cells themselves proved to be incredibly durable and to multiply faster than normal cancer cells.

Henrietta's highly unusual human cells are now used in scientific research all over the world. They were used to test the first polio vaccine and to study cancer and AIDS, as well as the nature of viruses, the effects of radiation on human cells and gene mapping. And that's just for starters. There are billions and billions of HeLa cells living and thriving in labs all over the world. Some scientists have even suggested that HeLa meets the criteria for a new unique species!

The Hayflick Limit

Unlike HeLa, most human cells eventually die after dividing a certain number of times. That number is called the Hayflick limit, named after American scientist Leonard Hayflick. After cells have reached this limit, they commit a form of suicide, called apoptosis.

Here's how it works. Chromosomes have tiny caps on their ends called telomeres. The telomeres protect the chromosomes and the genes they contain from damage. Every time a cell divides, bits of the telomeres get shaved off. They get shorter and shorter. When the telomeres get too short, they send a signal to other parts of the cell to self-destruct. Apoptosis begins.

Even though all cells have a Hayflick limit, they don't all die at the same rate. Some cells take longer to reach their Hayflick limit than others. That's in part thanks to the enzyme telomerase. It repairs telomeres, preventing them from shortening and sending out their signals telling cells to self-destruct. Cells with more telomerase will be able to divide more times and live longer than cells with less telomerase.

HELA CELLS: HOW THEY WORK

Since HeLa cells were derived from cancerous cells, they contain a more active version of telomerase. HeLa's telomeres don't shorten with each cell division, so they never get short enough to trigger apoptosis.

The cells can also divide more times and faster than most other cancer cells — every 22 hours compared to every 48 to 96 hours. Because HeLa cells can divide so many more times than normal, and never undergo apoptosis, they can live beyond the Hayflick limit. That's what makes them, yes, *immortal*.

Can the Hayflick Limit Help Vampires Cheat Death?

So what does cell death and the Hayflick limit have to do with vampires? Quite a lot.

To begin with, imagine that, like HeLa, a vampire's cells had extremely high telomerase levels. That would enable them to bypass the Hayflick limit and live far longer than normal.

A normal human cell can divide about 50 times. Now imagine that a vampire's cells with a high level of telomerase could divide four times more, say, 200 times. If so, a vampire would be able to live up to 488 years old — four times longer than the longest-lived human. And if their cells could divide 500 times? Then they'd be able to live up to 1220 years. But what if their cells had such efficient telomerase, like HeLa's, that the telomeres never shortened at all? The vampire would have achieved immortality.

Once the vampire had beaten the Hayflick limit, other vampirish traits could result, too. Think about how vampires are reputed to have powers of regeneration: they heal superfast from any injuries. Bypassing the Hayflick limit and rapid cell division could explain this trait. Cells that divide ultrafast could produce new tissue in the blink of an eye and — *snap!* — make wounds heal just as fast. It could also allow the body to replace worn-out or damaged cells so the vampire would always remain in the pink, no matter how pale his skin looked.

Magic Metamorphosis

Vampires are said to be able to transform into animals. Could Dracula do this downright batty trick? For real?

While there don't seem to be animals that can transform into completely different species, there are definitely ones that can *look* like different species.

Most amphibians, for example, morph into different shapes. Think of water-dwelling tadpoles, which grow into land-dwelling frogs. These two very different forms help them survive. Tadpoles feed on the plentiful and varied food sources found in water: algae, plankton and tiny insect larvae. But ponds and lakes are filled with predators. Growing lungs and legs lets frogs live on land. There, they can more easily escape danger. They can also take advantage of a different food source, such as — *thwak!* — flies.

0 to 6 weeks:
tadpole develops teeth as well as skin over the gills

6 to 9 weeks:
starts sprouting two rear legs

9 weeks:
resembles a small frog with a long tail

9 to 16 weeks:
gradually loses its tail and grows lungs and a tongue

16 weeks:
becomes an adult frog, able to breathe oxygen from the air and live on land

Leptin

How do these creatures transform, seemingly so magically? The secret is hormones. These chemical messengers trigger cell activity in plants and animals. Humans have more than 50 different types of hormones. One of them is leptin, the same hormone that triggers metamorphosis in frogs! In mammals, it regulates appetite. But what if the increased levels of leptin also affected a person like it affects frogs, triggering a metamorphosis? Could a person's arms morph into wings, like a bat's? (Don't count on it!)

Trance-Sylvania

Vampires are said to have an uncanny ability to control their victims. They use a penetrating gaze to draw people to them like moths to a very cold, very creepy flame.

How might they do this? One obvious answer is through hypnosis. A person in a hypnotic trance becomes more susceptible to the power of suggestion. A hypnotist is a person who is trained to be able to put others into a trance.

Hypnosis is very real. It is used by medical practitioners to help people overcome their fears or give up bad habits like smoking. Many people practice it on themselves as a way to relax. Others, such as stage magicians, invite people from the audience onstage to be hypnotized. They then make them do ridiculous (but harmless) things, such as cluck like chickens or act like they are stuck in a raging blizzard.

Here's how hypnosis works. First, the hypnotist might encourage you to fix your gaze on a single object, such as a swinging pocket watch. This gets you to tune out everything else around you and focus on what the hypnotist wants you to focus on — his voice, lulling you into a state of relaxation and trust. Or the hypnotist might walk you through a series of prompts ("Let your arms go heavy") and encourage you to visualize pleasant scenes to help you relax.

Once you're in a relaxed state, the hypnotist might give you a series of rapid commands. If you trust him, you might be more willing to do what you're told. Even if it's "Cluck like a chicken!"

So it's possible that a vampire's hypnotic gaze really could put you in a trance. And at that point, you better hope you had garlic bread for lunch!

What's Your Stake?

Now that you've sunk your teeth into vampire lore and science, what's your take? Could vampires really exist? Or are they merely myth-understood? Take the following quiz and collect a stake for each right answer. Then see if you're destined to be a vampire, a vampire hunter or — *gulp* — dinner!

1. The vampire empire was in:
a. Russia
b. Bulgaria and Romania
c. England

2. The vampire controversy was:
a. a fight between two world-famous vampires
b. when people believed vampires existed
c. when people thought drinking blood was healthy

3. Bloodletting was practiced to:
a. release demons
b. punish people
c. tell the future

4. HeLa cells are:
a. friendly
b. a type of prison
c. immortal

5. Vampires first grew fangs in:
a. 1845
b. 1897
c. 1957

6. The best defense against a vampire is:
a. garlic
b. tomatoes
c. a stake

7. Drinking lots of blood is toxic since it contains:
a. vampirase
b. telomerase
c. iron

8. Dracula did *not*:
a. change into a bat
b. sing opera in a rich baritone
c. sleep in a coffin

0–2 stakes   VAMPIRE VICTUALS — He wants to suck your blood ... and you'll be so transfixed by his hypnotic gaze, you'll agree to be his next neck! Luckily, you won't turn into a vampire yourself. You'll just feel a little drained.

3–5 stakes   VAMPIRE SLAYER — You've armed yourself with garlic, stakes, a good map of Bulgaria and a healthy dose of vampire lore. You're totally prepared to track down that fanged fiend and stick it to him.

6–8 stakes   REAL VAMPIRE! — You are charming, attractive and smart. Yet even so, people tend to avoid you. Perhaps you'd be more popular if you didn't chow down on your friends. In the meantime, invest in a better toothbrush.

Answers: 1. b, 2. b, 3. a, 4. c, 5. a, 6. c, 7. c, 8. b.

BIGFOOT

Definition: hairy, giant apelike creature, sometimes known as Sasquatch, that dwells in remote, occasionally mountainous regions. Probably nocturnal. *Definitely creepy!*

VERY, VERY TALL

HOO-HEE! STINKAROO!

ENORMOUS EYES

HAIRY

CAMERA SHY

WEIGHS ABOUT 225 KG (500 LB.)

HUMANLIKE GAIT

GINORMOUS FEET

The Great Big World of Bigfoot

Wait — did you see that? It ran through the trees over there. It was big — really big. And hairy. And it stunk like a dead opossum. Was it just a hefty hiker in need of a haircut and bath? Or was it the mysterious monster they call bigfoot?

It could be. Mysterious, wild, humanlike creatures like bigfoot have stomped through myths and legends all over the world for, well, ever.

1. **BIGFOOT (a.k.a. SASQUATCH):** *shy, hairy, giant mystery-monster that haunts the mountainous regions in and around California. First reported in 1811.*

2. **SKOOKUM:** *large, hairy, legendary race of cannibals living on Mount St. Helens in Oregon. The name comes from a Chinook word meaning "evil god of the woods."*

3. **YEREN:** *gentle, reddish- or white-haired creature from ancient Chinese legends about magical forest monsters and humanlike bears.*

4. **ALMA:** *humanlike creature of Russian legends, with long arms and reddish-gray hair. First reported in 1420.*

5. **YETI (a.k.a. ABOMINABLE SNOWMAN):** *mythical creature that lives in snowy, high-altitude regions of Nepal. Often seen carrying a large stone weapon. Doesn't speak, but makes an ominous whistling sound. First reported in 1925.*

6. **YOWIE (a.k.a. YAHOO):** *hairy man of the woods from Australian Aboriginal legends. Has extraordinarily long arms and backward-facing feet (so its tracks lead in the wrong direction!).*

A Long (and Hairy!) History

Bigfoot has a very long, very hairy history. The ancient Greek historian Agatharchides described wild non-people who lived in East Africa. The Roman historian Pliny the Elder described a race of *silvestres* in India who had humanlike bodies but were covered in fur, had fangs and couldn't speak. In 500 BCE, Hanno the Navigator told of meeting a tribe of hairy, humanlike savages in West Africa.

Throughout the Middle Ages, the idea of a wild man of the woods was hugely popular across Europe. He sometimes appeared as a mythical creature called a faun that is half human and half goat, or as a green man made out of plants.

What made these wild-man stories so popular? Myths about scary creatures may have arisen as campfire stories warning of the woods' true dangers. Woods and mountains were often home to bandits or hermits who did not want to be found (just like the outlaws in the story of Robin Hood).

It's also possible that "wild man of the woods" was a way to describe anyone living in an "uncivilized" way. When modern civilization began 10 000 years ago, and nomadic hunters and gatherers settled down to a life of farming, the new lifestyle competed with the old for land and resources. Perhaps wild-man stories were how the new farmers described those living in the old way.

Folk stories about mysterious man-beasts remained just that — stories — until the twentieth century. That's when reported sightings had people wondering, *Could bigfoot really exist?*

Bigfoot's Big Break

Bigfoot became an overnight celebrity in 1958 when Gerald Crew, a California construction worker, found a pair of gigantic footprints at his work site. He asked a friend to make plaster casts of them. He showed them to a newspaper reporter. The story spread like wildfire, and the first bigfoot hunters stampeded to the area. An entire industry was born.

Bigfoot's celebrity kicked it up a notch in 1967. Two men, Roger Patterson and Bob Gimlin, claimed to have accidentally caught bigfoot on film, again in California. Their short recording (less than four minutes) supposedly portrayed a female bigfoot loping through the forest. Many argued the film showed nothing but an actor in a gorilla suit. Just as many argued that it was impossible to create such a realistic costume.

The controversy made bigfoot a huge star. Television programs, movies, toys, board games, comic books, pinball games and even a delicious candy were based on the giant, hairy hero.

It wasn't until years later that evidence dispelled these bigfoot sightings as mere hoaxes. Those footprints found by Gerald Crew? They were phonies, created by a prankster named Ray Wallace. And in 2004, a man named Bob Heironimus confessed to having dressed in an apelike costume for Roger Patterson and Bob Gimlin's movie.

Monster Fact

In Skamania County, Washington, it is against the law to kill bigfoot.

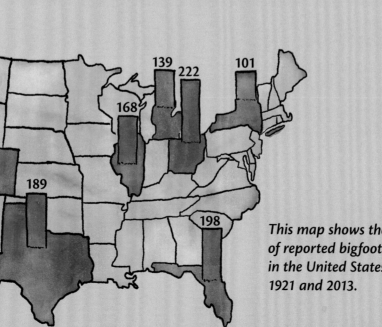

This map shows the locations of reported bigfoot sightings in the United States between 1921 and 2013.

ABOMINABLE HOAXES

We can't talk about bigfoot without talking about fakery, trickery and falsehood. The history of the enigmatic beast is riddled with made-up sightings.

- A hand, said to belong to a yeti, had been kept as a religious artifact in a monastery in Nepal. It was stolen in 1958 and passed on to movie star Jimmy Stewart, who smuggled it out of the country. In 2011, DNA testing revealed the hand was a fake, composed of human bones.

- During Sir Edmund Hillary's 1960 expedition to track the yeti, he came across a supposed yeti scalp in the same Nepalese monastery. When the scalp was sent for testing, it turned out to be made from the skin of a Himalayan antelope called a serow.

- In 2008, two men claimed to have found the body of a bigfoot in the woods of Georgia. They were paid $50 000 to tell their story. At a press conference, they revealed the body, preserved in a block of ice. The ice melted. The newly revealed corpse turned out to be nothing but a tricked-out Halloween costume stuffed with roadkill!

Why would people make this stuff up? Lots of reasons. In Nepal, some people say the locals tell stories about the yeti to keep tourists happy. Others like the attention they get when telling a wild story. And some do it just for money or for fun. There's nothing better than being in on a joke that others don't know about, is there?

Cryptic Cryptids

On your way home from school, you've spotted a mangy mutt. His fur is matted and (*pee-yew!*) he is in need of a serious bath. When the mutt's been scrubbed, shampooed and blow-dried to poodle-y perfection, you discover your new pet isn't a pooch at all ... he is one-hundred-percent mystery beast!

While it's hard to imagine, scientists discover mysterious new species all the time. Most are tiny microbes or insects. But it's possible that some larger animals, such as bigfoot (and your new pet!), remain to be identified.

Plants or animals that have not been officially identified and named are called cryptids. Technically, bigfoot would be considered a cryptid.

Many of the large animals we know today were only discovered and classified in the not-so-distant past. Perhaps Sasquatch will be next!

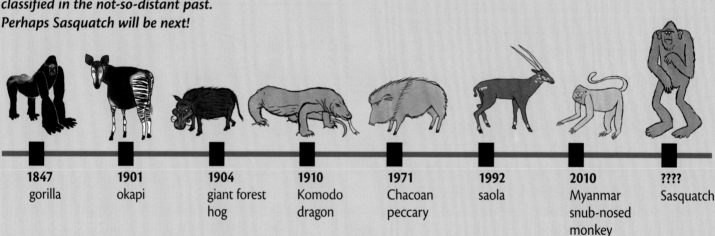

| 1847 gorilla | 1901 okapi | 1904 giant forest hog | 1910 Komodo dragon | 1971 Chacoan peccary | 1992 saola | 2010 Myanmar snub-nosed monkey | ???? Sasquatch |

CRYPTOZOOLOGISTS

Are you interested in hunting for bigfoot? Then consider a career as a cryptozoologist. Cryptozoologists are scientists who study and search for cryptids. The word *cryptozoology* comes from three Greek terms that mean "hidden," "animals" and "study."

Cryptozoologists study scientific subjects like biology or zoology. Fieldwork, where you observe animals in their natural habitats, would also be part of your training. Last but not least, brush up on your math skills. Cryptozoologists need to analyze plenty of data to separate fact from fiction.

Naming a Species

You might have decided to call your mysterious new pet Pooskie. When scientists discover a species, they also have to name it. The scientific naming of animals, or nomenclature, was a great contribution by Swedish naturalist Carl Linnaeus.

Certain guidelines make choosing the scientific name clear and easy. Each species on earth has a first and last name (just like you!). For example, your new pet's scientific name might be *Ursus pooskiesmellius*. The first part of the name (*Ursus*) states the organism's genus. Think of it as equivalent to your last name. The second part of the name (*pooskiesmellius*) identifies the unique species. Think of it as equivalent to your first name.

Linnaeus's Animal Classification

There are 1.2 million known species in the world — that's a lot to keep track of! So to classify, or group together, these plants and animals, we still use a system that was invented by Carl Linnaeus in 1758. The classification of plants and animals is called taxonomy.

Linnaeus's system divides living things into groups based on key features, such as whether or not an animal has a notochord (similar to a backbone). Each group splits into smaller categories.

While the taxonomic system is very useful, none of its categories are permanent. They change as scientists learn more about different organisms, how they evolved and how they are related.

Linnaeus's system was like an inverted pyramid, with the broadest group — the domain — at the top. As you move down the pyramid, the categories become more specific for each species. Here is what the taxonomic system looks like for the grizzly bear, Ursus arctos.

Domain 8+ million species	**Eukarya** (multicelled)	
Kingdom 1+ million species	**Animalia** (animals)	
Phylum 43 000+ species	**Chordata** (notochord)	
Class 5000+ species	**Mammalia** (mammals)	
Order 270+ species	**Carnivora** (mostly meat eaters)	
Family 8 species	**Ursidae** (bears and bear-like animals)	
Genus 4 species	*Ursus* (true bears)	
Species 1 species	*Ursus arctos* (grizzly bears)	

Sasquatchy Suspects

Assuming bigfoot and her kin are real, what might they be? Cryptozoologists have suggested the following Sasquatchy suspects.

Suspect #1: Not-So-Extinct Primates

In prehistoric times, a bigfoot-like creature definitely roamed the earth. *Gigantopithecus blacki* was a towering black ape that called the region now known as China home 125 000 years ago. It would have lived alongside our human ancestors but probably didn't pose much of a danger since bamboo was its main source of food. Bamboo doesn't grow in the mountains near California, so it's unlikely a surviving descendant of *G. blacki* would be found in bigfoot territory.

That doesn't mean another ancient primate couldn't survive there. Until about 30 000 to 40 000 years ago, more than one species of hominid — the class of animals that includes humans and our ancestors — walked the earth.

One early hominid was *Homo neanderthalensis*, or Neanderthals. Although they were a separate species, Neanderthals evolved from a common ancestor with humans. They are our closest extinct relative and were very similar to us: they used tools, made art and lived in nomadic bands as hunter-gatherers. But physically they were shorter, stockier and stronger, with different-shaped skulls.

Neanderthals lived in Europe and Asia from about 200 000 to 40 000 years ago. They eventually dwelled alongside humans and even interbred with us. Some genes found in people today have been traced to Neanderthals. These include the gene for red hair!

Homo sapiens

Homo neanderthalensis

Homo erectus

Homo heidelbergensis

Homo habilis

*This family tree shows how humans (*Homo sapiens*) and our relatives all evolved from a common ancestor (*Homo habilis*).*

What if Neanderthals didn't become extinct? Compare these facts to decide for yourself if Neanderthals and bigfoot are one and the same.

	Neanderthal	Bigfoot
Superstrength	✓	✓
Reddish hair	✓	✓
Communication skills	✓	?
Used fire and tools	✓	?
Lived in North America	✗	✓

WHAT IS EVOLUTION ANYWAY?

Human beings and our Neanderthal cousins shared a common, but now extinct, ancestor called *Homo heidelbergensis*. How we changed from our ancient ancestor to *us* happened through a natural process that occurs over a long period of time. It's called evolution. Charles Darwin was the first person to describe how evolution works in his groundbreaking book *On the Origin of Species*, published in 1859.

Darwin looked at traits, or characteristics, of species to see how they evolve over time. Certain traits, such as hair color, might not matter much when it comes to survival. Other traits can matter a lot. Imagine, for example, you are a kind of bird called a finch that lives on the remote islands of the Galapagos. On one of the islands, all the seeds have very hard shells. Only birds with strong beaks will be able to open them. Strong-beaked birds will survive and pass on their genes to the next generation. Their weaker-billed siblings, however, will starve and die out. Eventually, only finches with strong beaks will be living on that island.

Darwin called this process natural selection. He showed how it worked in many different species of animals, and he proposed that it was the main driver of evolution.

In his day, Darwin's theory was very controversial. Today, overwhelming evidence from many branches of science shows that natural selection is not only real but it is happening under our very noses!

Suspect #2: Misidentified Animals

Another possibility is that yetis and their kin are known animals that have been mistaken for mystery beasts. If so, it wouldn't be the first time!

A 1983 expedition to Nepal and Tibet uncovered yeti-like footprints. But the explorers were skeptical since they also heard vivid reports from local villagers of two types of bears. The researchers collected supposed yeti skulls from the area and compared them to skulls in several museum collections. The skulls turned out to match specimens from an Asiatic black bear.

A rigorous 2014 genetic analysis of 37 supposed yeti hair samples, collected from museums and individuals around the world, found that most were from known mammals, including polar bears, American black bears and raccoons! Two more controversial samples turned out to be most likely from the rare Himalayan brown bear.

In North America, grizzly or black bears are possible culprits in bigfoot sightings. Not only do they live in the exact areas that bigfoots are said to inhabit, but adult grizzlies or black bears look and behave a lot like bigfoots. When they stand up on their hind legs, they can reach up to 3 m (9.8 ft.) tall and can look like shaggy, smelly, giant people. Because grizzlies are also superintelligent, their actions can appear humanlike, especially if you spot one pawing through your camping gear in the dead of night.

Monster Fact

Research shows that young Asiatic black bears can create paw prints that look remarkably like human footprints.

Unusual Hybrids

It's a grizzly bear! No, it's a polar bear! No, it's a grolar bear! In 2006, scientists were surprised to discover a strange hybrid animal, a cross between a grizzly and a polar bear, in Canada's Northwest Territories. In 2010, a second grolar bear was found, this one a cross between a grizzly father and a grolar mother.

Researchers think the hybrid bears may become more common as climate change forces polar bears farther south into the grizzly bear's traditional territory. Maybe Sasquatches are really grolar bears or an entirely new hybrid!

Suspect #3: Wild Men of the Woods

Remember how, in the Middle Ages, outcasts and thieves sometimes lived in the woods? In every time and place, there are people who shun the company of others and prefer to live on their own, in the wild. One famous example is the case of the North Pond Hermit. He lived alone in a tent in the woods for 27 years and only ever talked to one person — a passing hiker (he said hi!). He never even lit a fire because of fear he'd be found. Perhaps bigfoots are really people like the North Pond Hermit who just prefer to be alone with nature.

Monster Fact

The name Sasquatch comes from a word that means "wild man" in the Halkomelem language.

"Wild" Child

Some wild people of the woods have been living that way their whole lives! Imagine a child lost in the woods, raised by wild animals. Wild, or feral, children like this do exist. Consider the following cases.

In the 1700s, a feral girl was found in France. She used her larger-than-average thumbs to dig up roots and she jumped from tree to tree like a squirrel.

Around 1912, a boy went missing from an Indian village where a leopard cub had been shot and killed. Three years later, the "leopard boy" was found in a cave along with two leopard cubs. Apparently he had been stolen by the leopard mother!

Another boy, Shamdeo, was found in India in 1972 when he was about four years old, playing with wolf cubs. His teeth were sharper than normal, and he ate raw meat and dirt. He was able to learn sign language but never learned to speak.

Could a "wild child" grow up to behave like bigfoot? It's certainly possible. But no one-hundred-percent verifiable case has ever been documented.

Mistaken Identity?

Not everyone who reports seeing bigfoot is a fraud. Some really believe they saw a giant, hairy monster running through the woods. But were their minds just playing tricks on them? Consider these reasons why seeing isn't always believing.

Confirmation Bias

It's snowing! Your best friend wants you to help her build a snowman. You think it's a waste of time — it's too cold out, and the snow is too dry. Sure enough, the snow you use to make the body won't stay together, and the poor snowman winds up a snow mess. Your friend blames you, saying you killed that snowman on purpose. But you swear you were doing your best. Who's right? Perhaps you both are. You may have thought you were doing your best, but your subconscious mind ("It's a waste of time") sabotaged the project.

Monster Fact

According to legend, spotting a yeti will lead to your death!

   In just this way, scientists' thoughts and feelings can subconsciously sabotage their projects. If this happens, it's called confirmation bias because a belief (bias) is confirming the outcome. In other words, if you expect to get a certain result, you might subconsciously manipulate the experiment so that the outcome matches what you expected. Your original beliefs are confirmed, but the results of the experiment aren't reliable. Scientists must take extra care to make sure their expectations don't affect an experiment's results.

The Power of Suggestion

Imagine your pal points and shouts "snake!" You look, and *EEK!* SNAKE! With heart a-pounding, you sneak another peek. Now you see … a twisty twig.

Would you have been snookered by the snakelike stick if your friend hadn't shouted "snake"? Probably not. The power of suggestion is superstrong. Advertisers rely on it. (How many times have you craved a hamburger after seeing a commercial featuring an especially juicy one?) Doctors rely on it, too, when they prescribe a placebo, a phony cure that really does make you feel better.

Sasquatch seekers can also succumb to the power of suggestion. Once people start reporting bigfoot sightings, others are more likely to "see" bigfoot, too — even if what they really saw was just a big, moss-covered log.

POWERFUL PLACEBOS

A placebo is a phony medicine — one designed to make you think you are being treated with, say, a powerful drug, when you are actually given something with little medicinal effect, such as sugar water. Placebos rely on the power of suggestion: if a patient believes he is taking a potent medicine, he may wind up feeling better, even if the placebo didn't contain real medicine.

It may sound crazy, but placebos really do work. In one study, heart patients were fitted with electronic pacemakers designed to keep their hearts beating normally. A second group got nonworking pacemakers but was told they received a working model. Three months later, *both* groups' hearts worked better than they did before they got the pacemakers. That's how powerful placebos can be!

The Power of Patterns

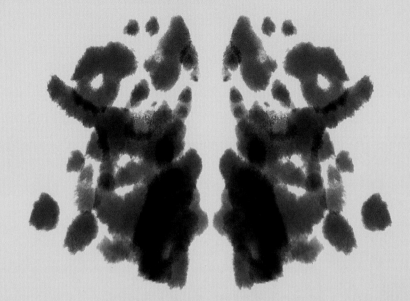

What do you see in this image? A pair of bats? A demon? A dancing bunny? That's not what the picture is supposed to be. It's not supposed to be anything! It's just a random splotch of ink. But the human mind loves to make sense out of things and create patterns where there are none. It will turn any random shape into a picture, if it can.

Now look at this image:

Do you see a face? We're especially good at detecting faces in random shapes. It's the pattern our human brains are most likely to form.

This pattern-making tendency may be at work in bigfoot sightings. Perhaps there's a tree stump in the distance, silhouetted against the sky. What first looked like bigfoot's beady eyes staring back at you might just be a random pattern on the bark. This effect is so common that tree planters in remote northern woods routinely refer to tree stumps in the distance as "bear stumps," since they are so frequently mistaken for grizzlies and other creatures.

Q: What do you get when you cross a yeti with a vampire?

A: Frostbite

Optical Illusions

Study the image to the right. Which orange dot is larger, the one on the top or the one on the bottom? You might be surprised to learn they are both the same size.

There's no mistaking that your eyes can fool you. When this happens, it's called an optical illusion.

Objects can sometimes look larger or smaller depending on their surroundings. Consider how you might look to an observer who saw you standing in the middle of a football field, as opposed to sitting on a tiny chair in a kindergarten classroom. How big or small things appear to be can also be affected by how dark or light it is, whether the horizon is visible or if there are shadows. Context clues like these help our brains understand what we are seeing.

Sasquatch sightings often take place where there are misleading context clues. Creatures might seem unusually large if they are standing in a grove of small, young trees (such as ones that grow after a forest fire) or if they are closer than you think because you can't see the horizon, which helps us gauge distance. Maybe this common optical illusion explains how a normal bear or person might appear gigantic in the deep, dark woods.

Memory

A frightened hiker reports a horrifying encounter with a mysterious beast. He might be telling the truth, but that doesn't mean what he describes was actually there. Extensive scientific research has shown that our memories are unreliable. Every time you retell a story, you actually rewrite the episode in your mind. You end up remembering the memory, not the actual event.

In a way, remembering an event is like opening a document on a computer. Every time you do it, a slight change is registered in your brain's hard drive. What's saved is no longer the original document, or memory, but rather the new version.

So that hiker might remember the scary-but-fuzzy mystery shape slightly different each time he recounts the story. Over time, he might believe it was a fuzzy Sasquatch that he absolutely, positively saw with his very own eyes.

BIGFOOT CROSSING

Sasquatch Survival Guide

Just because people can be fooled doesn't mean they always are. Sometimes campfire stories and the tricks that our eyes play are to warn us of real dangerous creatures in the deep, dark woods.

So what if bigfoot is more than just a story? Let's see how she would be able to survive in the toughest habitats of the world.

On Top of the World

All animals and humans need oxygen to survive. But yetis are said to live in remote mountains, where there is less oxygen at high altitudes. They would need to have adapted to live in such low-oxygen environments, like other beings who survive on high.

For example, residents of the Andes Mountains have higher concentrations of hemoglobin in their blood than most people. Hemoglobin is the compound that carries oxygen in the blood. Having higher levels lets people deliver more oxygen to their bodies' cells with each breath. That means they can survive and thrive in places where there is less oxygen in the air and where others would struggle for breath.

Monster Fact

Nearly 30 percent of Americans think that bigfoot is probably real.

HEMOGLOBIN: HOW IT WORKS

Hemoglobin is the molecule that carries oxygen through the blood in nearly all mammals. It is made up of a protein called globulin and iron-containing molecules called hemes. The iron in the hemes is what gives your blood its red color.

Iron has a special characteristic: it is able to bind with oxygen. Hemoglobin takes advantage of this fact by changing its shape or "state." In one state, oxygen is bound to the iron. It can then be carried throughout the body. When it arrives at the proper location, the hemoglobin physically changes its shape to release the oxygen.

The deer mouse, another native of the Andes, has a unique form of hemoglobin in its blood that is more efficient than other kinds. Maybe the yeti does, too!

BRRRigfoot

If you've ever hiked up a steep mountain, you'll have noticed it gets colder, and colder, and colder as you ascend. At very high altitudes — *brrrrrrr!* How could mountain-dwelling bigfoot cope with severe cold?

Being big would help. The larger warm-blooded animals are, the easier it is to stay warm. That's because they generate heat internally by converting most of the food they eat into energy. They then use that energy to maintain a constant internal body temperature. Compared to cold-blooded animals, such as reptiles, they need to eat much more food, relative to their size, in order to generate all that heat! The more volume warm-blooded animals have, the more heat they generate and the more food they need to eat.

Monster Fact

Bigfoot would need to occupy a territory the size of Chicago to find enough food to survive!

At the same time, larger animals have less skin, proportionally, for their size. This characteristic matters a lot in cold climates, because heat is lost through the skin. Small animals not only generate less heat than large ones, but they also lose it more rapidly.

So far, so good — bigfoot would have to be, well, big to stay warm. But size isn't everything. A toasty-warm fur coat would also help.

Hair, fur and feathers are terrific insulation. They work by trapping air next to the body. The trapped air is warmed by escaping heat. The warmed layer of air acts like a cozy invisible blanket.

Fat is also a good insulator. Seals, whales and walruses, for example, have thick layers of fat called blubber to keep them warm in cold water. Bigfoot would also have to have a thick layer of fat under his skin to survive in cold climates.

THE BIG POO STORY

Big, fat-bearing animals would also leave behind big fat piles of poo. Yet no one has ever found bigfoot feces. So the evidence, or lack thereof, suggests that the real bigfoot, if she existed, would be much smaller than legend suggests.

53

Sasquatch Hide-and-Seek

Now that you've chased down the facts of Sasquatch science, you can probably find bigfoot with your eyes closed! So test your knowledge by finding the answers that are hidden in this chapter. Give yourself one Sasquatch footprint for each correct answer, then check your score to see if you'll achieve fame as a bigfoot hunter or as a (*gulp!*) Sasquatch look-alike!

1. What animal is a cross between a grizzly and a polar bear?

2. What is an unidentified plant or animal called?

3. Who developed a system to classify living things?

4. Which species is our closest extinct relative?

5. What molecule carries oxygen through the blood?

6. What kind of eye trick could explain possible bigfoot sightings?

7. What did Darwin propose as the main driver of evolution?

8. What do you call a phony medicine that can have real effects?

0–2 footprints   BIGFOOT SURPRISE — What's big, hairy and staring back at you in the mirror? It's you — the hands-down winner of the Bigfoot Look-Alike Contest. Your prize? A hot bath, naturally.

3–5 footprints   SASQUATCH SEEKER — You're armed with a map of Northern California, a videocam, a hair-sampling kit and a poop-collector. You're ready to make history — as long as your folks don't make you come home before dark.

6–8 footprints   YETI DISCOVERER — You've found one! And it's alive! You coax your new furry friend down the mountain by promising it a grilled cheese sandwich with a side of coleslaw. Scientists name your discovery [*Your name here*] *smellius* — an entirely new species!

Answers: 1. grolar bear, 2. cryptid, 3. Carl Linnaeus, 4. Neanderthals, 5. hemoglobin, 6. optical illusion, 7. natural selection, 8. placebo

ZOMBIE

Description: undead corpse that rises from the grave to feast on human flesh. This walking dead has no thoughts, feelings or memories. It's focused on just one thing — chowing down on your *braaain*!

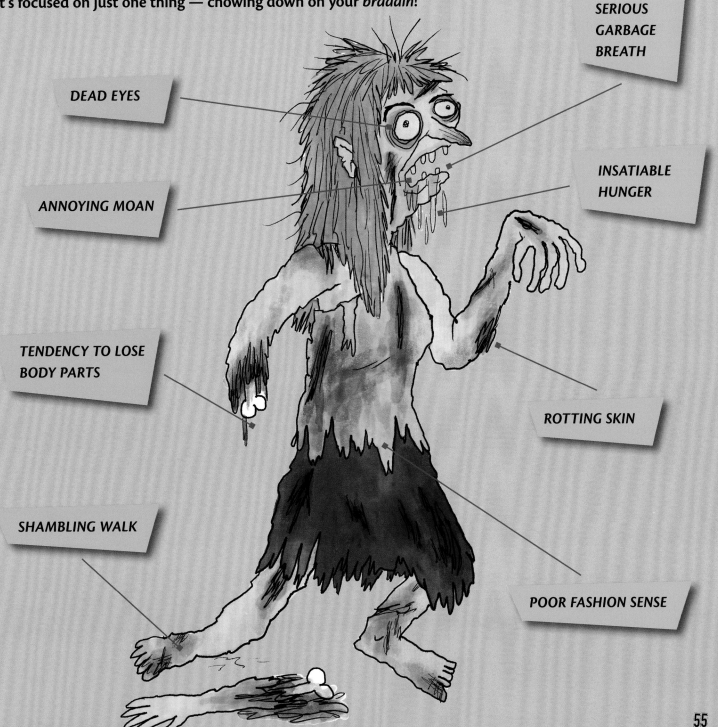

SERIOUS GARBAGE BREATH

DEAD EYES

INSATIABLE HUNGER

ANNOYING MOAN

TENDENCY TO LOSE BODY PARTS

ROTTING SKIN

SHAMBLING WALK

POOR FASHION SENSE

The Origin of the Zombie

You've had a late night, perhaps reading that creepy zombie comic under the covers. In the morning, you don't feel quite right. Your feet drag. Your eyelids sag. At the breakfast table, you respond to your family members with a pathetic moan.

Nowadays we might say you look like a zombie if you haven't gotten enough shut-eye, but where did that idea come from? It turns out that zombie history goes back hundreds of years. In 1685, King Louis XIV of France passed a law called the *Code Noir* (Black Code). The law stated that only the Roman Catholic religion could be practiced in France and its colonies — the lands that France had conquered and now ruled. Many of these colonies, like Haiti, were in the Caribbean.

There, vast plantations grew crops such as sugar cane. The plantation owners bought slaves who had been kidnapped from Africa to work on their plantations. Because of the *Code Noir*, the slaves on French-owned plantations had to convert to Catholicism, whether they wanted to or not. But many had their own religion, called vodun, which they kept practicing in secret. To disguise their rituals, the slaves incorporated Catholic symbols such as altars and candles.

Over time, a new religion evolved, called vodou or voodoo. It was practiced mostly in Haiti and in New Orleans, Louisiana. In the vodou religion, a bokor is a kind of priest or priestess who practices both white (good) and black (bad) magic. Many vodou worshippers believe that bokors can raise people from the dead. The dead will return as zonbis — with no memory and no will of their own — and become the bokor's slave!

Monster Fact

The word *zonbi* may have come from a word meaning "ghost" in Bantu, a language spoken in sub-Saharan Africa.

From Black Code to White Zombie

For hundreds of years, the belief in zonbis was confined to the French colonies. In 1929, though, word spread thanks to an American named William Seabrook, who published a travelogue called *The Magic Island*. The book described practices he claimed to have observed in Haiti, including vodun rites and what he called "zombies."

Seabrook's book inspired a popular 1932 film called *White Zombie*. Its plot revolved around an evil plantation owner who falls in love with a young woman. He obtains the help of a bokor called Murder Legendre to zombify her and make her his slave. The bokor then goes on to create many more zombies, who act as his own spellbound slaves and bodyguards.

Thanks to Hollywood, the notion of a zombie without a will of its own shambled to all corners of the world.

Night of the Living Zombie

The zombies in *White Zombie* were creepy but relatively harmless. In 1968, though, these mindless monsters suddenly became more hazardous to your health. That's when filmmaker George Romero made the blockbuster movie *Night of the Living Dead*.

Until then, all stories and films about zombies depicted living people enslaved by witch doctors. But *Night of the Living Dead*'s zombies were different: they were undead ghouls that fed on human flesh and blood. They weren't created by bokors or witch doctors. They were victims of an infection from outer space. Romero's zombies were inspired by Richard Matheson's book *I Am Legend*. It was about a bacterial infection that caused people to turn into another kind of monster — a vampire!

Romero's film started out as a cult favorite, but it became a worldwide phenomenon. Before long, there were dozens of books, movies, comic books and games inspired by Romero's vision. They ratcheted it up to the next level.

The old idea of the zombie was dead, and a new, more horrifying one was born.

Monster Fact

Zombies in popular culture didn't start eating brains until the 1985 movie *Return of the Living Dead*.

Real-World Zombies!

Meanwhile, back in Haiti, the old legends of bokor-created zonbis had never died. There were plenty of stories about real zonbis who roamed the countryside, doing their masters' bidding.

In 1982, Canadian anthropologist Wade Davis went to Haiti to find out if the stories were true. There, he met and interviewed Clairvius Narcisse, who claimed to have been a zonbi.

Narcisse had been pronounced dead in a hospital and buried in 1962. But in 1981, his sister saw him on the street, alive and well! He told her he'd been under the control of a bokor who fed him zonbi cucumber, a poisonous plant, to keep him in a dreamlike state. When the bokor died, Narcisse set out to restart his life.

Davis investigated Narcisse's story. He discovered a substance that could have caused Narcisse's symptoms. The secret "zombie powder" included toxic plants, pufferfish and charred, crushed human bones. The mixture caused paralysis and stopped the heart, simulating death. The victim who ate it would remain conscious but in a zombie-like state and unable to communicate.

Davis published his findings, but soon after his book came out, other scientists said zombie powders couldn't work that way. To this day, Davis's discoveries remain controversial.

Monster Fact

Animal brains are considered a delicacy in many parts of the world. In Cuba, sheep brains are fried into tasty fritters!

PUFFERFISH: A DEADLY DISH

Clairvius Narcisse was reportedly fed pufferfish to attain a zombie-like state. They may look Nemo cute, but pufferfish are extremely deadly. They contain a potent toxin called tetrodotoxin. If you eat enough, the poison first makes your tongue and lips go numb. Next, you feel tingling in your arms and legs. You may have trouble walking and feel sick to your stomach. Then comes the horrible part: you become paralyzed. You can't move or talk. You may find it hard to breathe. At high doses, you can even die within 20 minutes of eating the fiendish fish. One kind of pufferfish, or *fugu*, is a popular delicacy in Japan. Chefs must be specially licensed to prepare the fish dish. It's served with just enough toxic fish-flesh to make your lips tingle. Diners have died from accidental overdose while eating this dangerous dinner.

HUNGRY FOR HUMANS

For most people today, the idea of humans eating other humans, or cannibalism, is unthinkable. Yet cannibalism has been a part of human existence for at least 780 000 years.

There are many reasons why people have engaged in cannibalism:

- In Fiji, warriors believed eating human flesh prevented their enemies' souls from ascending to the spirit realm, where they could aid their tribe.

- The Iroquois in North America believed that if you consumed your enemies' flesh, you would gain their strength.

- In Central America, the Aztecs ate human sacrifices as a way to appease the gods.

- Members of the Wari tribe in South America thought eating their deceased relatives was a sign of respect and more humane than burying them in the cold, dark ground.

- Until the nineteenth century, people in Europe believed that eating certain parts of the human body could cure different ailments.

- In the Indonesian province of Papua, tribal people today still practice cannibalism as a ritual.

Whatever the reason, cannibalism wouldn't be good for you in the long run. Not only are human bodies too fatty to be part of a regular diet, but eating them can lead to a deadly disease called kuru.

A Bad Case of Zombie-itis

Imagine you're sitting next to the kid on the bus who's sneezing and coughing, sneezing and coughing. Sure enough, the next day, you feel that telltale tickle in the back of your throat. And by week's end, your whole family is down with the flu.

Now imagine what you caught is a zombie infection, like the one in *Night of the Living Dead*. Could that really happen? Could you actually catch a case of zombie-itis?

Infectious diseases have plagued humanity since the beginning of time. Some, like the common cold, are more annoying than harmful. But others can be downright deadly. A disease called Plague, or the Black Death, killed more than 100 million people during the Middle Ages. The Spanish flu epidemic killed 50 million people from 1918 to 1919.

When a new kind of infection develops and causes severe illness in a lot of people all over the world, it's called a pandemic.

THE PLAGUE: HOW IT SPREADS

The word *plague* is commonly used to refer to any terrible, contagious disease. But Plague (with a capital *P*) refers to a specific infectious disease caused by a bacterium called *Yersinia pestis*. It is found mainly in rodents and their fleas. If a person is bitten by an infected flea, the disease can cross into the human population. When it does, people get very sick, very fast.

Plague comes in three main forms:

The bubonic form causes flu-like symptoms, fever and swelling (called "bubo") of the lymph glands in the neck, armpits and groin.

The septicemic Plague occurs when the bacteria gets into the bloodstream. Patients wind up with severe abdominal pain and can go into shock. Some body tissues may die and turn black. That's how the Black Death got its name.

The third form is called pneumonic Plague. It affects the lungs. It is the rarest form but the deadliest — an infected person can die within two days if not treated immediately with antibiotics. Pneumonic Plague is also the most contagious. A cough or sneeze from an infected person is all it takes to spread the disease.

DEADLY DISEASES

Bacteria, viruses and other pathogens (things that cause disease) regularly mutate as part of the normal process of evolution. Their hosts — us — mutate, too. We adapt to them, and they to us, so both species can coexist happily. But once in a while, a pathogen mutates too quickly for our immune systems to adapt. People can't defend against the new bug. They get seriously sick. The result? A pandemic.

These real-life pathogens mutated in a way that caused pandemics in the distant — and not so distant — past:

- Tuberculosis (TB) has been dated as far back as the ancient Egyptians. Various forms affect different organs. One billion people have died of the disease in the last 200 years alone.

- Influenza (flu) pandemics were first reliably recorded in the sixteenth century. Potentially deadly strains of this shape-shifting killer spring up every year. That's why doctors regularly formulate new flu vaccines to combat them.

- Ebola was discovered in 1976 and is a highly contagious virus that causes fever and uncontrollable bleeding, painfully killing anywhere from 50 to 90 percent of its victims.

- The human immunodeficiency virus / acquired immune deficiency syndrome (HIV/AIDS) pandemic began in 1981 and has killed 39 million people to date. The disease hijacks the immune system so it can't fight off other infections.

- Severe acute respiratory syndrome (SARS) was first reported in Asia in 2003. It likely evolved from a bat virus and causes deadly pneumonia-like symptoms.

New diseases are evolving all the time. Medical researchers keep track of the symptoms to identify new diseases. Then they can develop vaccines or antibiotics to protect people from the infections and their worst symptoms.

Zombified Infections

Pandemics are real, and they do cause widespread disease and even death. But there's a big gap between catching the flu and becoming a zombie. Are there any real-world infections that could cause zombie-like behavior, such as losing your mind and becoming fixated on other people's brains?

Different types of parasites, viruses and prions can all do the gruesome trick. They can affect brain chemistry, causing their victims to go crazy and behave in monstrous ways.

These pseudo zombie-makers lurk where you least expect them. So don't leave the house without an ample supply of hand sanitizer!

Pesky Parasites

Parasites are organisms that live on or in another species (called the host). They attach themselves to their unwitting victim, and once in place, they suck nutrients from the host's body. They take nourishment without giving anything back, weakening the host. Eventually, the host might die. Then the parasite packs up and hunts for a new home.

Here are just a few examples of real-world parasites that control the brains of their unwilling hosts, causing zombie-like behavior.

Monster Fact

About 30 percent of people harbor the *Toxoplasmosa gondii* parasite. Just as it does in rats, it can alter brain chemistry in humans and cause reckless behavior.

A mind-controlling fungus called Ophiocordyceps unilateralis *forces ants to crawl down from their habitats and choose the perfect location to die. After the ant dies, a fungal stalk grows from the ant's head, releasing seedlike spores that infect its next victim.*

Unlike most creatures, Plagiorhynchus cylindraceus *loves to get eaten! That's how these spiny-headed worms invade their favorite hosts, including pill bugs. The worm affects the pill bug's brain, causing it to crawl to places where it will be eaten by birds — the parasite's other favorite host.*

Normal rats avoid cats like, well, the plague. But when Toxoplasmosa gondii *hijacks a rodent's brain and makes it reckless, it seeks out cats! When the infected rat gets gobbled up for dinner, the cat then becomes infected, too.*

Vile Viruses

Viruses are microscopic bits of DNA inside a protein coat. They are technically not alive, since they don't grow, eat or reproduce on their own. That changes when a virus finds its way into the cells of another organism. The virus hijacks the host cells. It morphs into a vile virus factory, spewing out millions of virus clones bent on death and destruction. Some viruses affect their hosts' brains, making them act in zombie-like ways that spread the viruses to new hosts.

Baculovirus zaps gypsy moth caterpillars. Once infected, the caterpillar climbs to a treetop, dies, decomposes and liquefies. As it melts, contagious caterpillar goo rains onto other caterpillars.

An infected animal transmits the rabies virus through its blood or frothy saliva. Unless you get a vaccine right away, you'll suffer confusion, agitation, uncontrolled mania and aggression. Within a few weeks of getting bit, you will bite the big one.

Petrifying Prions

Proteins are normally folded into specific shapes. Prions are abnormally folded proteins. They interfere with brain function. Eventually, the prions damage the brain so badly that it no longer works.

Experts aren't entirely sure what causes prions to form. Some think viruses could be a cause. Others think genes play a role. But experts agree: prions do cause zombie-like symptoms in animals and humans.

When infected by bovine spongiform encephalopathy (mad cow disease), a cow's brain develops sponge-like holes. Poor Bessie starts demonstrating classic zombie behavior: aggression, lack of coordination, staggering, drooling and teeth grinding.

Creutzfeldt-Jakob disease is the human equivalent of mad cow disease. You can get it by eating tainted beef from an infected cow. You wind up acting like crazy Bessie, too.

Could a Zombie Attack Really Happen?

According to legend, zombies are people who have died and then risen from the grave to become *un*dead. How could they accomplish this death-defying feat?

To date, there is no known way to revive truly dead organisms. Not even a little bit.

Once a living thing dies, the process of decay inevitably takes over. It's orderly, predictable and unavoidable. The only way to stop it would be to freeze the corpse.

Even if a zombie did come back to life and walk the earth, it would slowly decompose into goo. That would take about three weeks in a temperate climate, even less in the tropics. There'd be no chance of a zombie apocalypse if the zombies just rotted into slime, would there?

Process of Decay

The process of decay has five main stages. All of them are revolting.

1. Autolysis. Immediately after death, cells are still producing digestive enzymes. The cells get digested by their own products. The abdomen and veins discolor, and the body swells. YUK!

2. Putrefaction. Bacteria and fungi break down proteins, giving off a foul odor. The abdomen swells with gas, and skin begins to blister. EW!

3. Decay. Protein breakdown continues, along with carbohydrates and fats. Tissues soften, and organs and cavities begin to burst. Toenails and fingernails fall off. EEK!

4. Diagenesis. Any remaining tissue dies and hardens. The face becomes unrecognizable. Think: beef jerky. EGAD!

5. Skeletonization. The last remaining soft tissues decay or dry to the point where bones become visible. GAHH!!!

Monster Fact

Researchers determined that in the event of a real zombie outbreak, the entire human population would be wiped out in five to ten days!

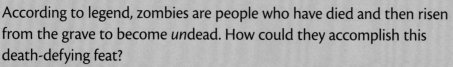

I'm Not Dead Yet!

It's winter and you're walking to school. Your best friend is heading your way. She's pale, and her skin looks clammy. Her eyes seem unfocused, and she's dragging one leg and zigzagging randomly. Has she died and come back to life as a zombie? And is she coming for you?

Probably not. More likely, she's suffering from hypothermia or another very real condition with zombie-like symptoms. There are even a few conditions that can make people appear dead when they decidedly aren't.

Remember tetrodotoxin and the bokor slaves? It turns out conditions that mimic death are much more common than you'd expect. Occasionally, people have been accidentally buried alive. Consider these shocking cases:

Monster Fact

George Washington was so afraid of being entombed alive that he made his servants keep him aboveground for at least three days after his constitution signed its last.

HAUNTED BY HORROR!!!

Count Michel de Karnice Karnicki, chamberlain to Tsar Nicholas II of Russia, never forgot the burial he'd attended of a friend's daughter. As earth was shoveled onto her coffin, the dead girl woke up! Karnicki was so traumatized by the eerie experience, he decided to make sure it would never happen again. In 1897, the clever count invented a safety coffin that had an air tube, a bell a victim could ring and a flag to wave.

THE SINGING REVEREND

Reverend Schwartz was a musical man. And a good thing, too. Because when he died in 1798, he was heard singing at his own funeral — from inside his coffin! He was taken out of the casket, alive and humming a happy tune. Once the ditty was done, so was Reverend Schwartz. He lay back down and gave up the ghost — this time for good.

THE CASE OF THE WOULD-BE JEWEL THIEF

In the early seventeenth century, grave robbers reportedly crept into the cemetery where the wealthy Marjorie Elphinstone had been recently buried with her best jewelry. When they dug her up, the bejeweled lady groaned in the ground! She nearly scared the wannabe thieves to death. Marjorie, awake and in possession of both her jewelry and faculties, walked home.

Burial vaults with internal escape hatches were built around 1890. If you were buried alive, you could unlock the cover from the inside. Just turn the handwheel!

65

Zombie Impostors

What might have caused dear Reverend Schwartz or poor Marjorie Elphinstone to appear dead when they weren't? A number of real-life medical conditions could explain their cases, as well as other conditions with zombie-like symptoms.

Hypothermia

Brrrr — hypothermia is when your body gets so cold, it can't work properly. At first, you find it hard to move. Your breathing slows and you might become clumsy and confused. Next, your blood vessels contract, making your skin go deathly pale. Your lips, ears, fingers and toes may turn blue, and your heart rate and blood pressure may drop so low, they'll be tricky to detect. Also expect trouble speaking, sluggish thoughts and amnesia; a staggering gait becomes common, too. If you don't get warm soon, your skin will become blue and puffy, walking will become impossible and you'll fall into a stupor.

Monster Fact

Cemetery headstones were originally used to keep the dead where they belonged — in the grave — in the event of a (rude) awakening.

Q: Why did the zombie do well on the test?
A: Because it was a no-brainer!

Cholera

This disease is nicknamed "the blue death" because extreme dehydration causes the victim's skin to turn bluish gray. It also makes victims appear really out of it. Bonus zombie effect — the disease is smelly (think diarrhea), highly contagious and really deadly.

Shock

This condition occurs when the body doesn't receive enough blood flow, and tissues and organs don't receive enough oxygen and nutrients. It can have the following death-mimicking symptoms: cool, clammy and mottled skin, especially on the hands and feet; shallow breathing; erratic heartbeat or absent pulse; hypothermia and swelling of the face.

Catalepsy

Catalepsy is a temporary state that can be caused by conditions such as Parkinson's disease, epilepsy, mental illness or withdrawal from certain drugs. Symptoms include rigid body, rigid limbs, loss of muscle control and reduced automatic functions, such as breathing.

BRAINPOWER: VOLUNTARY VS. INVOLUNTARY ACTION

Conditions like catalepsy happen when something goes awry with some of the automatic functions of the brain. While you might think you use most of your brain for thinking, the truth is most of it acts like your own personal autopilot.

Have you ever noticed, for example, how you don't have to think to pump blood through your body or to sweat to cool down? That's because these are involuntary actions — ones that our brains control automatically. But you do have to think to add two numbers together or decide when to raise your hand in class. These actions are called voluntary actions and require brainpower that isn't automatic.

Not surprisingly, each kind of action — voluntary and involuntary — is handled by different parts of the brain. The cerebrum controls all voluntary actions, while the cerebellum maintains both voluntary actions as well as involuntary ones such as balance, breathing and heart rate. If a person's cerebrum is damaged but the brain stem remains active, she may still be able to breathe and move without being conscious — just like a zombie.

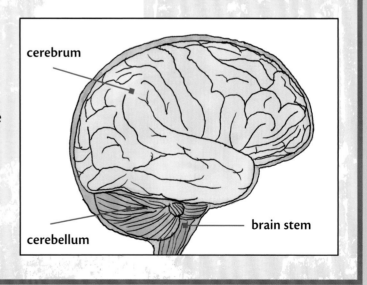

cerebrum

cerebellum

brain stem

Surviving the Zombie Apocalypse

Now that you're a zombie expert, it's time to test your skills in the field. Answer these true or false questions to see if you have the know-how to outwit the zombie horde. Then check your score to see if you would survive the zombie apocalypse or become a zombie yourself!

1. The Black Code was a law that made everyone dress in black.

2. Zombies originated in Haiti.

3. Bokors made zonbis out of fresh meat.

4. The best defense against a zombie attack is a toad.

5. *Night of the Living Dead* was the first movie to feature flesh-eating zombies.

6. Parasites can cause animals to act in zombie-like ways.

7. Prions are proteins that are folded to look like origami birds.

8. It is possible to come back from the dead.

9. Some medical conditions can make living people appear dead.

10. George Washington was afraid of being buried alive.

0–2 right	WALKING (UN)DEAD — Zombies have caught you, and you've caught a bad case of zombie-itis. Don't worry, you'll enjoy being a zombie. Since there will be no homework, you won't even need that missing eyeball.
3–6 right	SLIME SURVIVOR — You've managed to outwit and outlast the zombie horde. Congratulations! Too bad there's nothing left to eat except for (*eww!*) truly dead zombies.
7–10 right	ZOMBIE VICTOR — Not only have you survived the zombie apocalypse, you single-handedly ended it. As Benevolent World Dictator, your first order of business is burying all those smelly, rotting zombie bits.

Answers: 1. False, 2. True, 3. False, 4. False, 5. True, 6. True, 7. False, 8. False, 9. True, 10. True

WEREWOLF

Description: human being who turns into a ravenous, bloodthirsty wolf whenever the moon is full. In human form, werewolves usually look and act like everyone else. But as wolves, they're slavering after some nice, juicy bones — like YOURS!

HOWLS AT THE MOON

FEROCIOUS TEETH

GLOWING EYES

LOVES TO EAT MEAT ... NOM NOM!

NO TAIL

STRONG HIND LEGS

SHARP CLAWS

LARGER THAN YOUR AVERAGE WOLF

Werewolf Legends

The moon is full. You're feeling a bit out of sorts. Restless. Like you want to chase a car. And howl: *Arooo! Arooo!* Did you just eat a bad batch of wolfsbane? Or are you about to transform into — *eep!* — a werewolf?

Perhaps you're actually becoming a were-rabbit. Werewolves are only one possible kind of supernatural "were-animal." The Old English word *were* means "adult male human," so any creature with that prefix is said to be a hybrid man-animal.

Weirder than weird were-animals bound through legends and myths around the world. In India, for example, there are stories about were-tigers, in Africa people talk of were-hyenas and in South America tales exist about were-pumas and were-jaguars.

Were*wolf* stories, however, are the most famous were-tales of all. They mostly come from Europe, where, like zombies and voodoo in Haiti, they may have gotten their start in religious practices. In prehistoric times, boys endured tough initiations into warrior cults. These rites of passage involved wearing a wolf's skin, which people believed would magically transmit the animal's strength and ferocity to the young warrior.

Once Christianity began to spread throughout Europe in the fifth century, these warrior cult practices were suppressed. They even became associated with devil worship. Naturally, so did wolves. No wonder wolves became the stars of gory stories galore.

Monster Fact

Another name for a werewolf is *lycanthrope*. It comes from Greek words that mean "wolf" and "man."

WHAT'S UP WITH THE MOON?

The story goes that werewolves transform under the full moon. If so, that's just one of many strange powers ascribed to the moon.

For thousands of years, the full moon was thought to affect human behavior. It's said that during that time, both accident and murder rates increase, disasters are more common and people are more likely to behave in loony ways. In fact, the word *lunatic*, meaning an "insane person," comes from the Latin word *luna*, meaning "moon."

A hard look at lunar science sheds light on the moon's powerful physical effects on Earth. A full moon slightly increases global temperature. It also makes high tides even higher and low tides even lower. But there is no evidence that the moon affects people's behaviors or personalities. Scientific studies show that murder and accident rates *don't* go up during a full moon.

So would a werewolf at least howl at the moon? Not likely. Wolves howl to communicate with one another. They howl to announce it's time to meet up. They howl to let other wolves know where they are. And they howl to warn other wolves to stay out of their territory.

Wolves do howl more frequently at night. That's because they're nocturnal — they sleep during the day and are active at night. So they tend to get up to all kinds of wolfy behavior when it's dark, whether the moon is full or not. In fact, you are most likely to hear wolves howl at twilight and dawn, when they're hunting most intensely.

Wolves do lift their faces and howl up, up and away — in the direction of the moon. But that's because with their heads and throats in this position, the wolves can make the loudest sound that will travel the farthest.

The Inquisition

During the fifteenth and sixteenth centuries in Europe, werewolf accounts were no longer harmless tales. The continent was rife with superstition and suspicion.

On December 5, 1484, Pope Innocent VIII issued a ruling that said witches were real. He ordered church officials to root out and destroy them as heretics — enemies of the church. The pope's declaration, in part, fueled a period of terror known as the Inquisition.

Witches were widely believed to be able to shape-shift into other creatures. That's where werewolves come in: they were said to be witches who could shape-shift into wolves!

No one knows for sure how many suspected witches and werewolves were executed during the Inquisition, but best estimates range between 35 000 to 60 000 people. Eventually, witch and werewolf hunts fell out of favor. In England, the Witchcraft Act of 1735 made it illegal to accuse anyone of witchcraft or sorcery.

By the nineteenth century, only isolated pockets of believers still clung to the old superstitions. For most people, werewolves and witches became the stuff of make-believe and popular entertainment.

The Werewolf of Bedburg

One of the most notorious werewolf trials was that of Peter Stubbe of Bedburg, Germany, in 1589. Stubbe was caught red-handed — or red-pawed — when, according to his captors, he transformed from a wolf that was standing over its victim.

Stubbe was arrested and tortured. He then confessed to being a werewolf, saying that the devil had given him a magic belt made out of wolf fur that changed him into a greedy, devouring wolf.

Stubbe was convicted of 16 murders and executed. But was he really a werewolf? No one can say for sure.

Monster Fact

The 1941 movie *The Wolf Man* was a monster hit! It spawned a whole litter of spin-offs and influenced how werewolves were depicted in popular culture.

HOW TO STOP A WEREWOLF

Dozens of suspected werewolves were executed during the Inquisition. According to legend, the best way to kill a werewolf is with a silver bullet.

A regular bullet might work, too, depending on how good a shot you are. If you can damage the wolf's heart, brain or other vital organs, a regular bullet should do the trick. But most people are not that accurate. And perhaps a werewolf's hide is too thick for an ordinary bullet to pierce.

Silver, on the other hand, was considered a magical, purifying substance in ancient times. It could dispel evil and protect you from danger. Healers acted under the belief that "like heals like." If you suffered from a headache, for example, they might prescribe ground-up bits of human skulls for your cure. According to this principle, a cure for a condition *caused* by the moon — say, like becoming a werewolf — could be *cured* with a substance similar to the moon. Silver, which was traditionally associated with the moon because of its glistening color, was the obvious choice.

Today, silver lives up to the ancient claim that it can protect you from harm, or even heal you. It turns out that silver is a powerful antibiotic. It is toxic to bacteria that can make you sick. When silver was tested in small quantities in standard antibiotics, it boosted their bacteria-killing power up to a thousand times! And when small amounts of silver are added to water, it can kill many germs swimming in it, making it safer to drink. But in high quantities, silver can be toxic in the body — and so a silver bullet would provide a triple-strength weapon when shot at a werewolf's heart.

Could a Person Really Transform into a Werewolf?

According to legend, you can be transformed into a werewolf by several means: being bitten by a werewolf, surrendering to an evil curse, eating a mix of wolf and human flesh or wearing a wolf pelt.

But do any of these methods actually work?

Don't bet your last dollar on it. It's highly unlikely a complete transformation to another species could ever happen (see page 34).

What's more likely is that over time, a new type of hybrid animal, with features of both a wolf and a human, could evolve.

Hairy Hybrids

Imagine you could create a super pet that had all the characteristics of your favorite animals, like a turtlephant.

A hybrid is a cross between two separate but similar species — or between different varieties or breeds of the same species. The resulting offspring has qualities of both parents.

Hybrids are actually quite common in the animal world. One of the most well-known animal hybrids is the mule. A cross between a horse and a donkey, mules are thought to be stronger, smarter and easier to work with than either horses or donkeys.

But it's impossible for two very different species to form a hybrid because they are too different genetically. So you can hold off on adding a turtlephant to your wish list anytime soon.

Monster Fact

According to some legends, you can release a werewolf from his curse by either telling him he is a werewolf or calling him by his name.

Q: How do you make a werewolf laugh?
A: Feed him a funny bone!

Sheep and goats are genetically close enough to form a hybrid animal. A shoat — part sheep, part goat — really does exist!

Peas, Please!

One of the most famous experiments of all time had to do with hybrids — of peas! It was conducted by an Austrian monk named Gregor Mendel. He wanted to know how different traits were passed down from one plant to another. To find out, he crossbred, or hybridized, a variety of pea plants that had different characteristics and carefully recorded the offspring's traits.

Between 1856 and 1863, Mendel grew an estimated 28 000 pea plants! He found that in the hybrid offspring, certain characteristics — like yellow peas — were more common, or dominant. Other characteristics — like green peas — were less common, or recessive.

Mendel had discovered the laws of inheritance. Specific traits were passed from one generation to the next in ways he could measure and predict. But Mendel didn't know exactly how this information was passed along. It wasn't until 1900 that scientists learned that chromosomes are the agents of transmission, passing information from one cell to another.

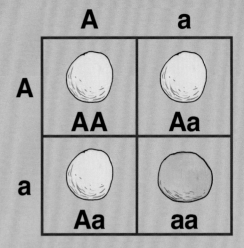

Biologists use a chart called a Punnett square to predict the traits of hybrid offspring. In this example, two peas are crossbred that each have a dominant yellow trait (A) and recessive green trait (a). Four outcomes are possible. Whenever the dominant yellow trait (A) is present, the offspring will display that trait and appear yellow.

CHROMOSOMES: HOW THEY WORK

A chromosome is a threadlike package of deoxyribonucleic acid (DNA) contained within the nucleus of the cell. The strand of DNA is made up of thousands upon thousands of individual units called genes. The genes tell cells what proteins to make. By doing so, they control every single cell function!

Chromosomes usually are found in identical paired sets. Different species have different numbers of them. Humans have 23 pairs, and wolves have 39 pairs.

Half of each pair comes from your mom, and the other half comes from your dad. The new set, however, is different from the set of either parent. Which genes it contains is determined by chance. One thing is certain, though — the new mixture is one-hundred-percent unique!

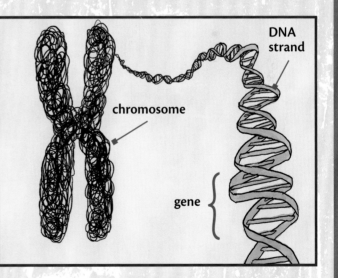

What About a Wolf-Human Hybrid?

For two species to be able to breed and create a hybrid, they must be very close genetically. *Homo sapiens* and our extinct relatives, the Neanderthals, were genetically close enough to interbreed (see page 44). But humans and the chimpanzee — one of our nearest relatives living today — are not. Even though we share 98.8 percent of our genes with chimps, as well as a common ancestor 13 million years ago, we have evolved too differently to get together.

(see page 44)

Monster Fact

The common ancestor of most mammals, including humans and dogs, was a furry insect-eater the size of a mouse called Boreoeutheria.

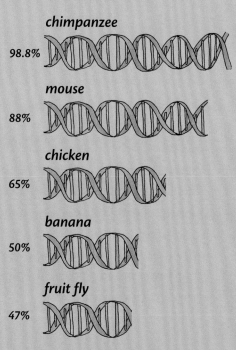

chimpanzee
98.8%

mouse
88%

chicken
65%

banana
50%

fruit fly
47%

Wolves and humans are even less closely related than humans and chimps. Our common ancestor lived more than 70 million years ago. Since then, humans and wolves have evolved in many different ways. Therefore, we are not genetically close enough to breed. Not, that is, without the help of genetic engineering.

Do you go bananas for bananas? Maybe that's because you're essentially a chimpanzee ... genetically speaking. Or maybe it's because you share half of your genes with bananas! Check out these species to see what percentage of genes you have in common.

Genetic Engineering

Times have really changed since Gregor Mendel's day. Not only do we now know that the DNA in a chromosome's genes is the agent of inheritance, but we know how to manipulate and change DNA inside individual cells. That process is called genetic engineering (see pages 18–19).

Scientists break open a strand of DNA using a chemical "knife" called an enzyme. They remove the desired genes. Then they insert those genes into the nucleus of another individual cell. The cell can be from the same species or, unlike hybrids, from a completely different one.

With genetic engineering, it would be possible, theoretically, to insert wolf genes into a human being's cells. That person would now carry wolf traits and be able to pass those traits to their offspring. Depending on which traits were inserted, they might have full luxuriant fur coats or sharp canine teeth! Then again, they might end up with an urge to chase squirrels.

Don't expect a wolf-human to be genetically engineered anytime soon. Rules about the ethics (the rights and wrongs) of experimenting on humans thankfully prevent even loony scientists from trying hair-raising experiments like this one.

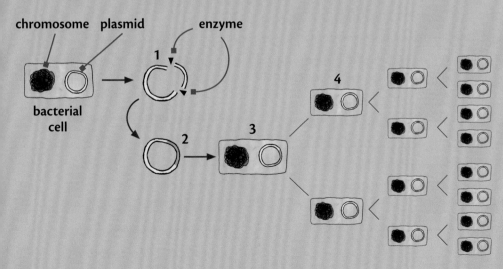

Scientists use genetic engineering to alter DNA. Here's how it works with bacteria:

1. *An enzyme is used as scissors to snip open the plasmid, a small piece of DNA.*

2. *A gene from another species is inserted into the plasmid.*

3. *The modified plasmid is inserted into another bacterium.*

4. *When that bacterium reproduces, the altered genetic information is passed to its offspring.*

77

Were-woof

But wait! A real wolf-human hybrid has been living among us for thousands of years. It prowls our homes and communities, slavering for any juicy hunk of meat it can get its paws on. It scratches at the back door, digs up buried bones and curls up, comfy-cozy, beside you on the sofa. It's — the family dog!

Dogs aren't genetically mixed with human beings. They are actually one-hundred-percent descended from wolves. But over thousands of years of living with humans, they've adapted to become very different from wolves. They are now a separate species.

That species has some surprising traits. Strange enough, some of those traits are uniquely human!

For example, dogs can read emotions on people's faces. Just like people, they usually look at the left side of a person's face, the side that tends to show emotions more clearly. Dogs may even be better than people at this face-reading skill!

If you've ever played fetch with Fido, you already know that dogs will look to where a person is pointing. No other animal can do this. Dogs have also evolved to understand human language.

As dogs adapted to us, we adapted to them. Studies show that most people can understand a dog's barks — especially ones that mean "ouch!," "watch it!" and "let's play!" We speak dog language, just as dogs speak ours.

So beware of the were-dog next time you call Fido to supper. He's licking his lips and turning into — you!

Monster Fact

Lupus erythematosus, a condition affecting the immune system, literally means "wolf redness." That's because in the eighteenth century, physicians thought it was caused by a wolf bite.

WOLFISH DISEASES

Throughout history, there have been many reports of people who behaved like wolf-human hybrids. During the early 1970s, a man was admitted to the hospital after he'd been caught sleeping in cemeteries and howling at the moon. Doctors performed a brain biopsy and discovered he suffered from a condition called walnut brain, in which the brain tissue deteriorates, leading to dementia and unusual behavior.

Walnut brain isn't the only condition that can cause werewolf-like behavior and appearance:

- Porphyria (see page 31) is a group of rare genetic disorders that causes light sensitivity, skin discoloration and flowy facial hair. Teeth, fingernails and the flesh beneath them can turn reddish brown. Sufferers can also experience mild hysteria or full-blown psychosis.

- Hypertrichosis, sometimes called wolfitis, is a hereditary disease that causes excessive hair growth all over the body — and, most noticeably, all over the face.

- Rabies is an infectious disease transmitted by the bite of infected animals, including dogs and wolves

(see page 63). It can cause aggression, rambunctious behavior and excessive drooling.

Many diseases cause symptoms that resemble werewolf traits. But do any cause a person to actually become a werewolf? Thankfully, not that we know of.

Werewolf Word Scramble

Now that you've wolfed down chunks of delicious science, you're probably becoming part wolf yourself. So test your knowledge by matching up the words on the left with the related words on the right. Then check your monster score to see how wolfish you really are.

1. lycanthrope
2. silver
3. witch
4. Mendel
5. hybrid
6. moon
7. Peter Stubbe
8. chromosomes
9. hypertrichosis
10. genetic

a. Werewolf of Bedburg
b. wolfitis
c. DNA
d. engineering
e. toxic
f. Inquisition
g. peas
h. tides
i. mule
j. wolf-man

0–2 right ONE-QUARTER WEREWOLF — You're a little hairy and a little smelly, but also only a little bit werewolf. The good news is you won't have to rush to the bathroom every ten minutes to comb your face.

3–6 right ONE-HALF WEREWOLF — You often get the urge to howl for no reason. But at the same time, you're thinking of becoming vegan. Taming your wild side is saving you from wolf despair. Trim your fingernails regularly.

7–10 right ONE-HUNDRED-PERCENT PURE WEREWOLF — You've already painted your bedroom black and stickered it with lots of stars and a big glowing moon. The real fun begins at the next full moon when you get to stay up way past your bedtime as your wolfish other half. The downside? It's gonna be lonely … since you ate all your pals last month.

Answers: 1. j, 2. e, 3. f, 4. g, 5. i, 6. h, 7. a, 8. c, 9. b, 10. d

SEA MONSTER

Description: any horrible, invariably huge creature that dwells in lakes, rivers or oceans. Feasts on ships, sailors and unwary swimmers, and enjoys playing hide-and-seek with frustrated photographers and unsuspecting prey (a.k.a. YOU!).

EXTREMELY ELUSIVE

Tales from the Sea

You're working on your front crawl in Lake Woeismee when you feel something brush against your butt. Is it a friendly fish, giving you a kiss on the cheek? Or … *something else?*

If deep, dark waters give you the jitters, you're not alone. Ever since people first began venturing out in boats, they feared the sea. And with good reason: the ocean was dangerous and unpredictable. Sailors who set out on voyages might be away from home for months at a time, or even years. Before radios and telephones, they had no way to communicate with the people back home. Ships could catch fire, be boarded by pirates or swamped in killer storms. Sailors frequently didn't return. Ever.

Naturally, people back home told dramatic stories to describe what had happened to the lost sailors. Sailors who survived the journey told tales, too, about the great sea creatures they battled. The stars of their stories took different shapes in different places. But they all shared one common trait — a taste for people meat!

Legendary Sea Creatures

Legends about sea monsters weren't simply make-believe. Coastal peoples knew that lots of strange creatures lurked under the waves — they dragged them up in their nets when they fished, or the creatures washed up on shore in huge stinking messes (imagine a beached whale …). No wonder stories about terrifying sea monsters were common all over the world.

Qalupalik is a creature from Inuit mythology that is a humanlike sea monster with green skin; long, tangled hair and witchlike fingernails. It hums ominously and snatches children when they are left on their own.

Selkies originated in Scottish, Irish and Icelandic folklore. They live as seals in the ocean but can shed their skin and live as humans on land. You can trap a selkie on land by stealing its skin.

Jörmungandr, or the Midgard Serpent, from Norse mythology is so large it surrounds the earth and can grasp its own tail. It's said that if he ever lets go of it, the world will end.

Sirens are from Greek mythology, and they sing so sweetly that no one can resist their voices. When you give in to temptation and try to approach them, your ship gets smashed to bits on the rocky coast.

Leviathan is a biblical sea monster that is 480 km (300 mi.) long, with glowing eyes and a powerful stench that no creature can endure. On its horns are the words "I am one of the meanest creatures that inhabit the sea."

Mermaids first appeared in Assyrian legends, but are common the world over. Their upper half is a human female, their lower half a fish's tail. They are associated with natural disasters, but sometimes help humans after falling in love with them.

Ryūjin is a mythical dragon from Japan that controls the tides. It lives in an undersea palace of red and white coral and has sea turtles, fish and jellyfish as its servants.

The Dragon Kings rule over the ocean in Chinese mythology. These four deities have five shaggy feet each, tipped with five sharp claws; glowing yellow scales and fiery breath that can boil fish.

Meet the World's Sea-lebrity Monsters

Hollywood movie stars aren't the only celebrities that are plagued by paparazzi. Wherever a sighting of an elusive sea monster is reported, curiosity-seekers come out in droves (and in very annoying boats equipped with loudspeakers) hoping to snap its photo. No wonder sea monsters get cranky. Perhaps all they want is a little peace and quiet.

Get up close and personal with these notorious A-listers below — even though they usually shun the red carpet. But be careful if you ask for an autograph. You might wind up in over your head ... literally!

Loch Ness Monster (a.k.a. Nessie)

Location: Loch Ness, Scotland
First Sighting: sixth century

More people have claimed to see the Loch Ness Monster than any other sea creature. Saint Columba is said to have first spotted the monster while it was attacking a man. Saint Columba commanded it to stop, and lo and behold, it did.

In 1933, a big-game hunter named Marmaduke Wetherell found footprints he was convinced were Nessie's. Scientists scrupulously examined the casts he had made. They determined the prints were made by an umbrella stand with a hippopotamus foot as its base.

Nessie leaped, or swam, into true celebrity in 1934, when a London doctor released his now-famous photograph. But on his deathbed, the doctor confessed the picture was a hoax.

In 1972, the corpse of a mysterious animal was removed from the loch by a team of zoologists. It weighed 1.5 tonnes (1.7 tons) and measured 4.9–5.5 m (16–18 ft.) long. Was it — *gasp* — Nessie? No. One of the zoologists had dumped a dead elephant seal into the loch to play a practical joke on his pals.

Kraken

Location: off the coasts of Iceland, Greenland and Norway
First Sighting: twelfth to thirteenth century

Tales of the kraken go back to Old Icelandic sagas. It was said that a terrifying squid-like monster named Lyngbakr would wrap its tentacles around a ship and snap it like a twig. It would then drag the broken ship (along with its screaming sailors) into its maw for a tasty, satisfying snack.

In 1874, a schooner called the *Pearl* was sunk by a giant squid, while passengers and crew on a nearby ship watched helplessly. Only four members of the crew and its captain survived the attack. The following year, the kraken was spotted again, this time in battle with a sperm whale. In 1930, the kraken supposedly attacked a Norwegian navy ship called the *Brunswick* three times. The crew reported that the monster rammed the ship and wrapped its tentacles around the hull. It couldn't hang on to the slippery steel, though, and fell off — right into the ship's propellers.

Monster Fact

One of Hollywood's most famous monsters is Gill-man from the 1954 classic film *Creature from the Black Lagoon*.

Champ

Location: Lake Champlain, bordering New York, Vermont and Quebec
First Sighting: 1609

The French explorer Samuel de Champlain was one of the first Europeans to describe Champ. Or, rather, to describe a monstrously large fish that resembled a pike. However, a lake monster was already part of the Native lore in the region long before Sammy showed up. The Abenaki people called the creature Tatoskok. The Iroquois called it Chousarou. Later it would be described as a sea serpent with the head of a horse.

By the late nineteenth century, Champ had become such a popular tourist attraction that P. T. Barnum, a circus owner and showman, offered a $50 000 reward for evidence that Champ was real. He wanted Champ's carcass to display as an attraction at his world's fair. Barnum's show went on without Champ, and Champ remains a mysterious denizen of Lake Champlain.

Uncharted Waters

If you've ever gone beachcombing, you know that strange, fascinating objects wash up on the beach all the time. You can't help but wonder where these mysterious mementos came from and what other treasures — or creatures — might turn up on the sandy shore.

You wouldn't be the first person to want to know more. People have been trying to explore the oceans and learn about its creatures for thousands of years. But before sonar was invented in 1917, no one had any idea how deep the deepest parts of the ocean were.

Today, marine biologists and oceanographers use sophisticated tools such as sonar and small submarines to search beneath the waves. While researchers have gained oceanic amounts of knowledge, even more remains to be discovered. More than 95 percent of the ocean has never been explored. No one knows what lives in those vast reaches of the sea!

If sea monsters did exist, they would probably dwell in the deepest, darkest parts of the ocean. That's where many undiscovered animals live, in what we call the ocean trenches.

1.2 million identified species

7.5 million unidentified species

An estimated 8.7 million species live on earth, but only 1.2 million have been identified. That leaves a whopping 7.5 million species that have yet to be found — and most of them live in the ocean!

Sonar: How It Works

Sonar (short for Sound Navigation and Ranging) is a technology that lets you find out the distance and shape of objects by bouncing sound waves off them and listening for the returning echo.

A sonar transmitter on a ship creates a pulse of sound, called a ping. It can be either a single, constant frequency or a changing frequency, known as a chirp. The sound waves spread through the water. When they hit an object, they are reflected back toward the sonar receiver.

The speed of sound through water is affected by several factors, including salinity (salt levels), depth and temperature. This information is combined with the length of time it took to receive the echo to calculate the object's distance.

By sending more than one ping at the same object and examining the angles at which the reflected waves return, operators can also figure out the size and shape of the target object.

Ocean Trenches

When scientists began using sonar to map the ocean floor, they got a huge shock: there was an underwater mountain range encircling the whole globe. At 60 000 km (40 000 mi.) long — that's like running around the world 1.5 times! — the mid-oceanic ridge system is the biggest geological feature on the planet.

Scientists wanted to understand how the mountains got there. With further exploration and experimentation, they learned that the earth's crust is made up of several large plates that rest on a layer of molten rock, called magma. The magma is constantly moving and pushes the plates in different directions. Sometimes they meet and crash together, forming giant mountains. At other times, they force one plate under the other. Deep gashes, called ocean trenches, open in the earth's crust.

When we say ocean trenches are deep, we mean deep! The Marianas Trench is almost 11.27 km (7 mi.) deep — that's nearly 2.5 km (1.5 mi.) more than the height of Mount Everest!

These undersea canyons are pitch-black and home to an incredible variety of life, including giant tube worms, eyeless shrimp, enormous mussels and crusty crabs. Together, these bizarre critters form a complete food chain in the darkest reaches of the ocean. They are one-hundred-percent real … and one-hundred-percent (*yikes!!!*) creepy creatures of the deep.

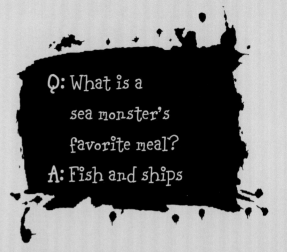

Q: What is a sea monster's favorite meal?
A: Fish and ships

A creepy collection of critters makes their home in the ocean's basement, at the bottom of deep ocean trenches.

Could Sea Monsters Really Exist?

Deep down, most people fear the unknown. And nothing is more unknowable than mysterious monsters lurking in the ocean depths. No wonder sea monsters have been trawling through people's nightmares for centuries. But do they really swim the seven seas? And if so ... what are they? Cryptozoologists, or scientists who search for new species, offer a few suggestions for likely suspects.

Suspect #1: Not-So-Extinct Animals

In the past, real animals that resemble modern-day descriptions of Nessie and Champ swam the seas. Most are now extinct ... or so people believe.

Plesiosaurs were giant, cold-blooded reptiles that lived between 215 and 65 million years ago. They had huge, rounded or humped bodies, flippers, long necks and small heads. The largest known plesiosaur, the *Elasmosaurus*, was bigger than a school bus.

Basilosaurus was the most common ancient whale. It lived between 40 and 35 million years ago. It had a wedge-shaped head and a narrow, streamlined body that resembled a sea serpent. Is it possible that these supposedly extinct marine animals have managed to survive, mostly unnoticed, in the briny depths?

A Basilosaurus could grow up to 23 m (75 ft.) long. That's longer than a lane at a bowling alley!

Consider these unusual cases. The coelacanth is an ugly deep-sea fish that was widely believed to be extinct. But in 1938, a live coelacanth was caught off the coast of South Africa. And in 2010, two carcasses of the fabled spade-toothed beaked whale — the "rarest whale in the world" — washed up on a New Zealand beach. To this day, no one has ever seen one alive!

What if a plesiosaur was also able to survive undetected? Could this ancient sea creature actually be Nessie? A deeper comparison helps us separate the facts from the fathoms.

A second coelacanth specimen was identified in 1952.

Plesiosaurs in the Waters of Loch Ness?

Plesiosaurs were cold-blooded reptiles. They lived in warm, tropical waters.

The waters of Loch Ness are too cold for a reptile. The average temperature is only about 5.5°C (42°F).

Plesiosaurs were so large they needed huge amounts of food.

Loch Ness is too small to provide enough food for these mammoth beasts.

Plesiosaurs lived millions of years ago.

Loch Ness was created during the last ice age, about 10 000 years ago. It was dry land before that, so there is no way an ancient ocean species could have gotten trapped there.

Plesiosaurs were air-breathing animals. That means they likely had to surface several times a day to breathe.

Loch Ness is a smallish lake, so there would be ample opportunity to spot an air-breathing sea creature … yet no one ever has.

WARM-BLOODED VS. COLD-BLOODED CREATURES

Whether you are playing softball in the summer sun or skiing down a frosty slope, the inside of your body will probably stay a constant, comfy 37°C (98.6°F). That's because human beings, like other mammals and birds, are warm-blooded (endothermic). We use energy from the food we eat to maintain a steady internal temperature.

Reptiles, on the other hand, are cold-blooded (ectothermic). They can't generate their own body heat. They rely on outside temperatures to keep them warm. If temperatures are too cool — roughly, below 10°C (50°F) — they can't maintain body processes or even move their muscles! That is why most species of aquatic reptiles (such as sea turtles, crocodiles and water snakes — and such as plesiosaurs, back in the day) live in the tropics, where both water and air temperature remain warm year-round.

Suspect #2: A Case of Mistaken Identity

You've got a new school assignment: researching plesiosaurs. Your first stop might be the library, or you might search the web for fascinating facts. But when Nessie was first spotted in the sixth century, Saint Columba didn't have the internet. He would have had to use the information at hand to figure out mysteries, like what that strange beast was rising from the loch. Not only was it harder to access information back in Saint Columba's day, but much less was known about sea dwellers than we know now.

Since then, many thousands of animals have been reported, described and identified. There are plenty of possible contenders for the role of most frightening and entirely real sea monster. This gruesome gallery of undersea rogues offers up just a few possibilities.

Monster Fact

People in medieval times believed that land animals had underwater counterparts, such as horses and sea horses. Sea bishops and sea monks were the marine mirrors to humans!

Frilled Shark

This shark's monstrous appearance is enough to frighten even the most sea-hardened sailor. Its needlelike teeth and projecting jaws make it a fearsome-looking predator.

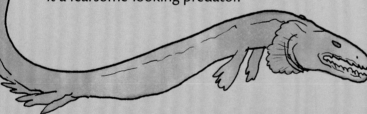

Basking Shark

When this creature dies and its long body washes up on shore, its gills rot quickly. That leaves behind a carcass with an unusually long "neck" that looks very sea serpent, indeed!

Oarfish

This rarely seen eel-like species of long, bony fish lives in deep waters. Along its back is a row of about 400 spiky dorsal fins that look like teeth that ripple through the water. On its head are even longer, spikier fins.

Blue Whale

These giants are the largest known animal in the world and can grow up to 27 m (89 ft.). They weigh about the same as 35 elephants! And their calls are even louder than the fiery roar made by a launching space shuttle!

Supersized Squid

The best candidate for a real-life sea monster is the giant squid (*Architeuthis dux*). Even though reports of its existence date back to ancient Greece, this ginormous creature was only seen alive in its native habitat for the first time in 2004. A live specimen was brought to the surface in 2006. It measured 7.3 m (24 ft.) long, but the species can grow up to 13 m (43 ft.) in length — that's bigger than a four-story building!

Giant squids have eight thick arms and two extra-long feeding tentacles. Each arm is covered with hundreds of powerful sharp-toothed suckers, measuring 5 cm (2 in.) across, a little bigger than a Ping-Pong ball. The long tentacles can zing out and snag prey from up to 10 m (33 ft.) away! The squid then draws lunch into its mouth using its arms. A sharp beak at the opening of its mouth slices the prey into bite-sized pieces.

Giant squid are so large the adults have few predators. But there is at least one animal capable of catching and eating a giant squid — the sperm whale. Squid parts have been found in the stomachs of sperm whales, and the skin of sperm whales is occasionally marked by squid suckers — evidence of what may have been an epic battle to the death. Perhaps stories of kraken attacking ships were actually cases of giant squids that mistook the ship for Moby Dick.

Some scientists think there may be as many as eight different sub-species of giant squid! This might explain the many different descriptions of kraken-like sea creatures throughout history. And both the kraken and the giant squid share a common characteristic: a voracious appetite! The giant squid, like all members of the Cephalopod family, have relatively short lives. These supersized specimens probably live less than five years. To grow so huge in so short a time, they must eat enormous quantities of food. Ships and sailors might have seemed to them like a nice light snack.

Monster Fact

The name *kraken* comes from a Norse word meaning "deformed" or "twisted."

Monster Fact

The giant squid has some of the largest eyes in the animal kingdom. They can measure up to 28 cm (11 in.) in diameter — that's about the same size as your head!

Suspect #3: Monstrous Phenomena

Did you see that? Something was moving down there ... in the water!

Hold your sea horses. Just because the water is moving in a suspicious way doesn't mean there is something lurking below. There are a number of natural events that can explain those strange ripples.

Consider these natural phenomena and how they might inspire the stories of terrifying monsters under the sea.

Tsunamis

Remember Jörmungandr, the Norse serpent so large it could wrap itself around the whole world? Or Leviathan, the sea monster that was 480 km (300 mi.) long? Imagine the splash a creature that big might make when it dives beneath the surface. It would be so big, it might create a monster wave!

Monster waves, or tsunamis, do occasionally form in the ocean. They can grow so large they swallow entire coastlines. Perhaps Leviathan has something to do with them. But there's also a scientific explanation for those big waves.

Tsunamis are caused by earthquakes or other disturbances deep in the ocean. An underwater earthquake can move the ocean floor straight up! That motion creates a wave that can travel for long distances and gain enormous height as it approaches the shore.

When the waves hit land, they do so with devastating power. Anything in their path gets tossed or smashed — which is exactly what happened when devastating tsunamis hit parts of Asia in 2004 and again in 2011.

Tsunamis can be truly monstrous. That's why modern tsunami warning systems have been invented. By measuring earthquakes under the sea and wave height changes in the open ocean, scientists can predict when possible tsunamis may strike and alert people in time to clear out.

Monster Fact

The largest tsunami ever recorded struck Lituya Bay, Alaska, in 1958. It measured a staggering 524 m (1720 ft.) high. That's as tall as 300 people standing on one another's shoulders!

Whirlpools

Whirlpools are water currents that spin in a circle, sucking in anything nearby. You've probably seen one when you drain the bathtub. The whirlpool during bath time isn't anything to be scared of, but getting out of a whirlpool at sea is very difficult. That's because you'd be fighting against both the force of the swirling water and the pull of gravity.

In the ocean, whirlpools are usually caused by tides and the way water behaves when it crashes against the coast. The most powerful whirlpools form in narrow, shallow straits. The Saltstraumen whirlpool in Norway reaches speeds of 37 km/h (23 m.p.h.), while the Old Sow off the coast of New Brunswick has been clocked at up to 27.6 km/h (17.1 m.p.h.).

These whirlpools are powerful enough to overturn a small boat — like in many sea monster tales — although it's unlikely that a whirlpool could suck down an entire ship.

Seiches

There's something rippling, rippling there — in the water. You blink and rub your eyes, but when you look again, it's still there! What else can it be but Nessie?

It could be another kind of monster wave called a seiche. It's sometimes called a "standing wave" because it can stand in one place for hours — or even days!

Seiches can form in large bodies of partially enclosed water, such as lakes or reservoirs, as a result of changes in air pressure and wind during a storm. A single large wave, or a series of them, can resemble humps in the water. Under the right conditions, they can look a lot like Nessie or Champ.

Monster Fact

In Greek mythology, Charybdis was a monster that would swallow down the waters and spit them out again. It's now believed that a whirlpool in the Straits of Messina, in Southern Italy, inspired the myth.

Sea Monster Sink or Swim

You've traveled to the bottom of Davy Jones's locker and come eyeball-to-eyeball with some of the scariest sea monsters ever described. Are you ready to test your knowledge and see how you would fare on the open ocean? Read the statements below and decide if they are true or false. Then check your monster score to see if you would sink or swim on the high seas.

1. The Loch Ness Monster is probably a *Basilosaurus*.
2. The giant squid has the largest eyeballs in the world.
3. Champ was first described by the world heavyweight boxing champion in 1902.
4. Saint Columba stopped the Loch Ness Monster from killing a man in the sixth century.
5. A seiche is a standing wave.
6. Sonar is used to detect underwater objects.
7. Reptiles cannot generate their own body heat.
8. The spade-toothed beaked whale would be easy to catch.
9. More than 95 percent of the world's oceans are unexplored.
10. No creature could survive in the pitch-black ocean trenches.

0–2 right   DAVY JONES — You are a born landlubber. Giant squids would take one look at you and lick their lips … if they had lips. Avoid all bodies of water, even rain puddles. They may be home to your arch enemy, *Waterius drownius*.

3–6 right   SAMUEL DE CHAMPLAIN — You are a born seafarer and explorer. You have nothing to fear from sea monsters. Unless, of course, you fear being eaten alive. Stick to shallow water.

7–10 right   LEVIATHAN — You are the greatest sea monster of them all. So great, in fact, you can live on land. No wonder no one has ever been able to spot you in Loch Ness or Lake Champlain. You're busy sinking toy boats in the bathtub (*mwa ha ha*).

Answers: 1. False, 2. True, 3. False, 4. False, 5. True, 6. True, 7. True, 8. False, 9. True, 10. False

Index